PEACE YOUR WAY TO SUCCESS

KENISHA HANSON

PEACE YOUR WAY TO SUCCESS

A Foundational Guide to Cultivate Peace,
Prioritize Yourself, and Achieve Your Goals

Perceptive Peace Publishing
2022

Kenisha Hanson © 2022

All rights reserved.
No part of this book may be reproduced, stored, or transmitted by any means- whether auditory, graphic, mechanical, or electronic- without written permission of both publisher and author, except in the case of brief excerpts used in critical articles and certain other noncommercial uses permitted by copyright law. Unauthorized reproduction of any part of this work is illegal and is punishable by law.

ISBN: 978-1-7388336-2-7

Because of the dynamic nature of the internet, any web addresses or links contained in this book may have changed since publication and may no longer be valid. The views expressed in this work are solely those of the author and do not necessarily reflect the views of the publisher, and the publisher disclaims any responsibility for them.

Printed in Canada
Perceptive Peace Publishing, 2022

Visit www.peaceandsuccess.com
to access your free resource kit and help you to start taking immediate action toward your peace of mind and success.

Tag me on Instagram @thekenishahanson.
and share your favorite resource.

DEDICATION

You are greater than you ever could imagine.
It is time to curate the life you deserve and thrive in peace.

TABLE OF CONTENTS

Dedication 5
Introduction: Thrive in Peace 9

Part One: Finances 17
Chapter 1: Getting Personal 19
Chapter 2: Empower Yourself 25
Chapter 3: Career Alignment 32

Part Two: Mental Well-Being 37
Chapter 4: Allow Yourself In 39
Chapter 5: Higher Power 47

Part Three: Interconnections 55
Chapter 6: Know Your Presence 57
Chapter 7: Friends and Family 61
Chapter 8: Romantic Relationships 66

Part Four: Physical Health 73
Chapter 9: Physical Story 75
Chapter 10: Health Check 80
Chapter 11: Environmental Shift 85

Part Five: Success 91
Chapter 12: Maintain Your Peace 93
Chapter 13: Success Story.. 100
Chapter 14: Redefining Success 107

Epilogue.. 119
Peace Your Way to Success Reflections 124
Peace Your Way to Success Affirmations 134
Message From the Author 141
Acknowledgment.. 143
Author Bio 145
Synopsis 153

INTRODUCTION:
THRIVE IN PEACE

Welcome to *Peace Your Way to Success: A Foundational Guide to Cultivate Peace, Prioritize Yourself, and Achieve your Goals*. Thank you for purchasing this book. My hope is by the time you reach the end of this book, you will have the practical tools to evaluate your own life and make the necessary adjustments that align with your peace and give you the clarity to achieve your goals.

We all go through challenges, hardships, obstacles, or inconveniences that try to take our will to succeed. For some reason, it seems as though when you're ambitious—which I am sure you are because you picked up this book—you experience moments when you cannot seem to catch a break. This shakes you a bit, and sometimes, you want to (or maybe you do for a moment) throw in the towel, yet the desire to achieve your goals remains inside you. I want to congratulate you on choosing yourself at this moment to learn something that may help you get closer to your dreams and your peace. To prioritize yourself is to know and love yourself. It is understanding your needs, wants, and desires and articulating them confidently. It is showing up for you.

This book will allow you to evaluate the key areas of your life to determine if your actions and inactions align with your goals and values. Through alignment, you obtain peace, and through peace, you receive clarity and the mental capacity to move through whatever life throws at you in the pursuit of your dreams.

I am writing this book in 2022, and now, more than ever, you might feel like you're being pulled in countless directions, bombarded with never-ending to-do lists, and subjected to overwhelming negativity from various sources, including the media, others, and even your own inner critic. If this resonates with you, chances are you fall into one of the following categories or perhaps a combination. You're likely someone with profound commitment and unwavering drive, always ready to shoulder the burdens of others. However, at times, you might find yourself with less than what you truly need, and a lot less than you deserve. People around you may perceive you as the go-to person, someone they can always rely on, the strong one who seems invincible. But let's face the truth: you're only human, and there are limits to what you can bear and how much you can do. Time and time again, you've stretched yourself thin, and your hyper-independence often hinders you from asking for help, no matter how much you need it. Lately, it feels like things are slipping out of control, and despite appearances, you don't have it all figured out – you just carry the load exceptionally well, maybe even too well.

Or perhaps you are diligently striving to pursue your goals—or so it seems. In reality, you may be engaging in busy work, tasks that, while they appear to align with your goal, don't contribute significantly to making real progress. You only have so much mental capacity at the end of the day to actually do something meaningful. You give so much of yourself, often taking on the burdens of others, and in the process, your own happiness starts to slip away bit by bit. Over time, you realize that people have pushed past your boundaries, and you've sacrificed many of your own needs, with everything on your personal to-do list remaining untouched. Yet, despite your exhaustion, you continue to push forward because you feel you have a lot to live up to, and deep down, you're convinced there must be a way because the dreams you have never seem to fade.

Then there are those of you who have achieved a goal you set out to attain, only to find yourself overwhelmed and unfulfilled. You checked all the boxes, did all the right things, but something is missing. Consequently, a new, even bigger goal looms on the horizon, and you believe this will finally bring you the contentment you seek. However, chances are it won't, because if you're anything like me, that dream or goal was never truly yours, or perhaps it was, but circumstances changed along the way. Yet, you never pause to check in and see if it aligns with the current version of yourself. This can lead to confusion and a cycle where you keep moving the goalpost, continually attaching your happiness to a future achievement.

When we neglect to pause, tune into our self-awareness, and evaluate our own needs, we'll keep satisfying the needs of others, leaving ourselves spinning in a perpetual cycle, with our peace and happiness trapped in the distant future. The good news is that I understand these emotions, which is precisely why I wrote this book.

Living in a perpetual state of internal chaos, misalignment, and mental exhaustion doesn't serve our well-being or our progress in life. Despite the North American hustle culture, I can assure you that it does not have to be this way. I also want you to know that this book is neither overly complicated, nor am I here to fill you with extreme positivity. Life presents challenges, and it's not my intent to minimize your experience. Instead, my aim is to provide an actionable plan grounded in practical tools that support you holistically while also giving you the space to adapt it to meet your needs. I'm here to help you clarify your goals and guide you in living in alignment with them. I'll empower you to reflect on your needs and desires so that you can consistently prioritize yourself and live a life peacefully designed by you.

What's my story? Growing up, I always had a curious mind. I loved journaling and reflecting on who I was and what the things were that were happening in my life. I was described as happy, optimistic, quite particular and kind. As I grew up, I was everyone's go-to person. I helped everyone with everything at any time. However, I now realize that many of my seemingly positive characteristics were due to feeling like I did not belong. This resulted in me constantly extending and overextending kindness to others, trying to include people, so they never felt what I felt deep inside. I was fortunate enough to thrive in the school environment. I loved getting good grades, and I loved playing sports. I was on every team, and when I was not on a team, I was in the chess club or the model cars club. I attribute much of this to overcompensation due to my feelings of inadequacy. I felt I was not enough, or I had to do more to be worthy of my father's love. My parents were no longer together, and it felt like I had to do more to earn his presence. I also never wanted to disappoint my mom because I knew how much she did to support us each and every day. It was us against the world.

Introduction: Thrive in Peace

In 2018 our lives changed when she became suddenly ill and completely paralyzed with a rare condition called Neuromyelitis Optica (NMO). I watched her in pain every day, and I became a full-time caregiver before the age of 30. I deferred my overseas admission to get a PhD in hopes of attending school the following year. The following year, I was diagnosed with Stage IV Hodgkin's Lymphoma. It all felt like a joke, and I was convinced that it couldn't be real. I was healthy, active, and doing everything I thought I should be.

At that moment, I knew I could blame myself and my circumstances and fall into the darkest of places, or I could prove that everything I had done and experienced thus far was to prepare for this moment. It was a tough reality, but I knew I didn't want to get stuck in the mud. I had to keep going. I had to show up for myself in every way because no one else could conquer this battle for me. I am happy to say that I am in remission now. I have redefined my success and acquired even bigger dreams. I transitioned from law enforcement to a corporate career, and I am an entrepreneur, author, and certified personal development coach. I have learned to meet life with ease and evaluate how I am preserving my peace in every facet of my life.

The purpose of *Peace Your Way to Success* is to empower you to have your own system to cultivate peace in the key areas of your life, so you can have the mental capacity to achieve your goals. Prioritizing your needs prepares you for whatever may come and allows you to persevere and thrive in the present. My life after cancer has refined how I show up for myself, and I constantly curate how I want to experience life. All that I do is for my inner peace, and anything that doesn't align with that needs to be evaluated, with a commitment to the appropriate action. Situations, life, and people will drain you if you let them.

Hyper-independence is exhausting and so is being the strong one all the time. It's up to you and no one else to know what is not working for you. No one truly can save you from yourself.

I refer to "for my inner peace" as a reminder to realign myself with what I need, but it also serves as a reminder to evaluate the key areas of my life:

Finances: What is the current state of my finances? What is depleting me, and what am I doing well?

Mental: What story have I told myself about my abilities or my situation? Am I making time for activities that bring me peace, joy and fulfillment?

Interconnections: Do my friends, family, or significant other drain or support me? How can I cultivate more meaningful connections in my life?

Physical: Am I prioritizing my physical health through diet and exercise? How can I create a supportive and healthy physical environment for myself?

The purpose of this book is not for you to read it and to put it back on your shelf. It's a reflective process, which takes work—consistent work. Thus, you may have to return to it a few times to get it right or focus on one area that challenges you the most. Use it how you need to use it and do what supports you. You may want to utilize the resources provided or even reach out to me to help you on this journey.

Introduction: Thrive in Peace

> *Visit peaceandsuccess.com to access your free action guide to support your success journey or reach out to me at connect@kenishahanson.com*

I chose to use my cancer story not to garner sympathy or position this as a tragedy but to highlight the urgency to act. I also wanted to emphasize the unpredictability of life and empower you to take an inventory. Sift through the facets of your own life and determine what is serving you or depleting you while making the necessary adjustments. I understand that none of this is easy, and that reflecting on and choosing yourself feels like one of the most difficult things to do. This could explain why we prefer to go through the motions and get to our own "stuff" later and for some, never.

Maybe there is guilt or fear in prioritizing your needs, perhaps the reactions of others, or you fear that you will feel less of a mom, friend, or loved one. I struggled with this as well, but I also observed the internal frustrations or resentment that led to irritability and caused me to show up as a less desirable version of myself. The truth is that showing up for yourself serves you and everyone else around you. You can achieve all that you want and experience the life you desire, but it starts with internal work. It starts with cultivating your peace of mind, so you can thrive in this chapter of your life and the next.

PART ONE
FINANCES

CHAPTER 1:

GETTING PERSONAL

"Money can't buy happiness, but poverty can't buy anything."
—Unknown

Have you ever stopped to question your money story? Where did you learn about money? How are you with money? How do you view people with money? How do you want your future self to be with money?

I asked these questions because it took me some time and digging to understand what they meant. I didn't really understand my money story or where I picked up my money habits. When I took a closer look, I realized I learned a lot from my environment and upbringing in a single-parent household.

My mom worked hard, sometimes long hours, and she often was frustrated because she had to rely on public transportation. We lived in city housing at the time, a cooperative housing complex, and I loved it. I had no idea what housing meant, but I knew I got to go to day camp and get Christmas boxes and other fun things through government assistance. What I didn't know was how hard my mom was working to move out and own a home of her own. I always had what I needed and a couple things I wanted. Not to mention that when I visited two of my three sisters from my father's side who lived in the suburbs, they usually had more than enough for me to play with.

At the end of grade eight, during my basketball season while I was preparing to go to high school, my mom had other plans—we moved to the suburbs, what I considered a city kids nightmare. Naturally, that was an extremely tough time for me (or so I felt) because I no longer would be with my friends. Drama ensued, and I cried and cried, stating that I did not want to go. Needless to say, none of my ocean full of tears made a difference; we moved away, and everything changed.

When we first moved, we slept on a mattress on the floor in front of a heater, and I remember wondering to myself, *why did we move out here for this?* Maybe I wondered this because I was older then, but it felt like we had less. Sometimes, my mom didn't have enough to cover the bills, and she would be stressed because she was "short." I didn't understand it then, but I knew things had changed.

This is where my money story started forming. I had to help my mom because it was just us. If I didn't help her when she was short, who would? I knew my mom was independent. Some would say she was hyper-independent, and asking people for help was not something she liked. This translated into my just-in-case or saving for a rainy-day story because that rain was always just around the corner. I learned that I always had to prepare for an emergency because not having enough seemed like a pretty stressful situation. There was only one problem; I didn't have a job. I promised myself that when I got a job, it would be different. I didn't understand why there was sometimes not enough, but I knew I didn't want it to happen anymore. When I got my first job at a gas station cafe and throughout my adulthood, I maintained this story. I was always pretty responsible with money, and I ensured that I always had some money saved should my mom need help. The older I got, the more I saved because, well, just in case. Also, it gave me peace knowing that I was prepared for whatever may come.

Then, it happened. The just in case was before us in the form of a full-on emergency. When my mom suddenly fell ill and was left completely paralyzed in 2018, I realized we had made vastly different financial decisions. Her money story was different from my story. My mom immigrated to Canada when she was incredibly young, and she had little support into her teenage years. She had to figure a lot out on her own, and she did. She went from a shelter to housing to owning her own home and a car in the suburbs. The financial decisions along the way were not always pretty because there was survival wrapped up in there. I never had to worry as much about survival, and for that, I am grateful.

With all the cards on the table, there was a level of vulnerability, exposure, and powerlessness that occurred in a short time for her because she was a nurse making almost six figures with six-figure financial commitments. As the months went on, and she was still in the hospital, it became more and more apparent that her finances were now my responsibility. I had done everything right or the best that I could, and now, I got to inherit all the financial decisions of my mother. I remember being extremely frustrated when I was approached for money at the hospital by a lady she worked with. The lady was the lead of the partner draw (think of it as a cultural community savings partnership) that my mom had been a part of for years, and sometimes, we did it together. The lady was freaking out about $100 or whatever it was, and I couldn't believe it. I told her I was paying for everything else and would pay for her share until it was over, and she just continued to go on about needing this money. I respectfully exited the conversation because if I couldn't afford to give her $100.00, I would have much bigger problems. Luckily, there were only two more payments, and I just gave her everything at once and did not engage with her any further. Maybe it was nothing, but it felt like everything at the time. There was a lot going on for me, and this felt like salt in a wound. I didn't know if my mom would be okay or if she would ever walk again and I was being pressed for $100.00 as though that was my greatest concern. My current reality may have been why I was really frustrated. I understand the partner lady had to make sure that other participants got their share of the money, but I said I had it and there was little tact and compassion for someone she claimed was a friend.

Truly the only thing that saved me in that time when I had to assume all the expenses of almost a six-figure woman was the fact that my own expenses were extremely low. I didn't have very many outstanding expenses, just regular recurring bills. I learned then that the financial decisions you make don't just affect you; they also can affect your loved ones, the ones with whom you live, or the ones with whom you're close to. Life is unpredictable. I find, at least in my experience, that sometimes for Black women or immigrant families, you often have to care for or provide for your family or extended family in some capacity, which means the decisions you make and the ones they make affect you. How are your current expenses? Could you survive six months or even three months without your income?

Chapter 1: Getting Personal

> *Visit peaceandsuccess.com to access this free resource:*
> *Monthly Expenses Calculator*

The story you have formed about money can dictate what you do and how you do it. This story may have a positive or negative influence on your money habits. It is up to you to figure out what works and what doesn't work. Sometimes, those around you simply don't know enough, or they don't share enough for you to get all the knowledge you need. What is certain is that money and a perceived or real lack of it disrupts our peace of mind. We also receive many conflicting messages about money. We are told, "Money is the root of all evil, or money can't buy happiness." Still, I can assure you that poverty or the threat of poverty and the inability to meet your basic needs such as food, shelter, and safety is not a place of contentment.

Being open about money and the ways you spend it can be uncomfortable, even if the conversation is just with yourself. Something happens inside, and shame, comparison, and other emotions arise. I have experienced it and told myself how much I should have by now or wondered how people my age or younger than me afford all these things. Still, none of that is my business, and you never know what people have to go through to get money and maintain it. Moreover, how much of what you see is actually what they have? The "should" story was created by someone else out there, and what the Joneses are doing (referring to Keeping Up with the Joneses) doesn't serve you; it serves them. Where you are now doesn't dictate where you will be unless you let it. You can give yourself a new story. I had to tell myself that I am capable of understanding finances, and I am deserving of wealth to start changing the scarcity mindset that I had developed. We are all operating from our own lenses, experiences, advantages, and disadvantages. Offer yourself grace. Show up for yourself and begin changing the trajectory of your life.

If this speaks to you, I want you to take the time and be honest with yourself and your relationship with money. Where did you learn your money habits, and are they currently working for you? In what ways do you want to improve?

Reflections

1. Evaluate your money story for your starting point. It's okay not to have it right. However, acknowledging and understanding what you want and don't know are the first steps to improving your situation.
2. It's okay to go outside your networks and learn information. Think about where you can go to improve your knowledge. Saving for an emergency fund was only one part of my finances; I had to figure out what was next.
3. In what area of your personal finances are you skilled, or what do you want to learn more about?

CHAPTER 2:

EMPOWER YOURSELF

"Investment in knowledge pays the best interest."
—Benjamin Franklin

What do you know about personal finances? What do you want to know? What have you learned in the past year?

As I mentioned before, I didn't know much about money. I just knew I didn't want to run out of it or come up short in an emergency. Although I knew nothing about what happens when you have good credit, I always heard adults talking about making ends meet and bad credit, and knew I wanted good credit.

One day, I had a conversation with an adult family member. I started to make more money in a senior position, and I was trying to understand all the different things I was now paying into. I was talking about benefits, pensions, and retirement savings, and to my surprise, we started contributing to our pensions at the same time. They began explaining why they were not contributing previously, and honestly, it sounded like stories and excuses. I thought to myself, *you needn't justify your decisions to me. Your retirement age is on the horizon, and they want me to work another 30 years (which is not happening)*. I had an assortment of questions because that person, too, worked for the government, so my relative was afforded a lot of these same benefits, but I realized that they didn't seem to know much or maybe just chose to not utilize much of what was offered. Politely, I let the conversation fade into the background.

I guess there's a point in your life when you realize that adults don't always have it all together. They're just older than you. I realized I had a decision to make—to continue in my ignorance and blame those around me or figure it out. I chose to figure it out, but where was I going to get the information? I had to start somewhere, so I made an actionable New Year's resolution—not the fleeting one's people make each year. I was going to make learning about finances a priority in 2019.

Interestingly, in reflecting on my money story, I also realized that I always felt that I could not excel in the area of finances because I was not good at math. From an early age, I struggled with it, but I was a girl, and I was smart in everything else, so there really was not a push from me to get better. Then, in grade 10, academic math came along and confirmed everything I thought. I barely passed the class, and I elected to go to summer school to only get 2% higher. What I didn't realize was how much that steered my career path and interest. I never thought about business, finance, or economics because there was no way I could do that if I couldn't understand slopes. However, it was time to reevaluate that story and commit to my new resolution because I knew something was missing; there was so much I did not know. I was starting to save a lot more, and I had a decent amount in my account that was just sitting there with no idea what to do with it. Therefore, I went "old school" and headed to the library to get books on personal finance. What an adventure that was. If you want to know just how much you don't know, take a trip to the library. It can humble the greatest of minds.

It was overwhelming at first because the library had so many books that I didn't know where to start, but I needed to know what I didn't know. I did not want to look back at all I could and should have done. I wanted to make informed decisions. I wanted to feel empowered about my decisions. I wanted to be a boss, and I wanted to be aware of what was happening with my money. I wanted to have these conversations and understand what they were talking about when my grandmother flips the channel to CNN. I took out many different books and started with short beginner ones with digestible language. I didn't need to be a pro and master this in a day, but I did want to have a good foundation.

One of the books discussed the pros and cons of a financial advisor and fee structures should I decide to get one. I am not here to advise you to do anything with your finances; my only advice is to be informed. You should know why you're doing something, what the alternatives are, and what it will cost you with or without the service.

Let's get back into it. I knew I was at a point where I wanted more, and I wanted someone with more education and knowledge in this area than I had. As I mentioned, one of the books I borrowed broke down how to evaluate choosing a financial advisor. I went on to interview a couple based on what the criteria were that were listed, what my needs were, and where I was on my journey. I selected the right advisor for me, and it was an empowering experience that brought me so much peace and confidence. Like, I did that! My advisor is a person of integrity and a family woman who wants most for her clients to succeed, specifically women of color, which resonated with me and my needs. One thing I didn't expect was that my financial advisor combed through my workplace benefits and policies to determine what coverage I had and what I would be eligible for in varying circumstances. Naturally, I told all my friends and family all that I had learned; some took the time to evaluate their own needs, while others did not. However, life has taught me that it is not my responsibility to ensure they act but to give the information, so they can act if they choose.

> *Visit peaceandsuccess.com to access this free resource:*
> *Benefits Analyses*

I now have a portfolio with investment accounts, dedicated contributions, and an understanding of the stock market. More importantly, I have insurance. My financial advisor informed me that it was great that I had all this money, and I was doing so well on my own, but there was no point in having it if I didn't protect my wealth. The wealthiest individuals have insurance policies, and much of their generational wealth is created through these policies. I had a decent life insurance policy that I maxed out through my employer. Still, my advisor said we would take out something small in the event that I transition jobs, or there's a gap in my employment. Some people may think of it as someone pushing insurance, but I have seen how life can change suddenly, and again, it's crucial to make informed decisions. My advisor also said it's important for me to have critical incident insurance in the event that something happens that prevents me from working. This could be a car accident, broken limbs, illness, or just any ailment that puts people in positions where they can no longer work for an extended period, with several categories on how much they get based on the severity of the claim. There was no need to convince me here; I already saw what happened to my mom.

What I didn't know was that I would need to claim critical incident insurance so soon, and that same year, I would receive my cancer diagnosis. The unfortunate part of this story is that I was deemed ineligible because the first time I went to the hospital I was in the ineligibility window. In this instance, I did what I was supposed to do. I got the critical incident insurance, but when I had THE critical incident, I was not able to claim it because I was a few days shy of the eligibility window. It was too close to when my policy began. My advisor went back and forth with the insurance. My doctor got involved, and nothing happened. I was ineligible. I wish I could say I was angry, but at that point, it was sad and comical all at the same time. This is the time that I would need it. I only could hope that stage four cancer would be the most critical incident that I would experience in my lifetime, but unfortunately, I have learned that nothing is off the table.

I have to think of it like this. At least I have an external policy. After checking the cancer box, you likely will have to pay significantly higher premiums due to pre-existing health conditions, and it would make add-ons like critical incident insurance a challenge. While it is unfortunate (extremely unfortunate) that I didn't get the financial support to help me get through my treatment, I am prepared for anything else that may come.

The future is so unbelievably unpredictable. In order to have wealth, you must start by protecting it, creating a generational safe safety net so the burden is not on you or your family. I know it's challenging with the information age in which we live, and it sometimes can do us a disservice. Empower yourself by learning and committing to immediate action.

Where do we start? We're so bombarded with so much knowledge and opinions. It's easy to get overwhelmed. However, because it's the information age, it's not enough to say that we don't know if we claim to want more for ourselves. We must do more, and we must take action.

Take a moment to reflect on your financial knowledge.

Reflections

1. Identify what you want to know. Educate yourself with some baseline knowledge and seek out experts or take the time to learn for yourself.
2. Identify how you want to learn and commit yourself to immediate action. If my paperwork had gone through a few days earlier. I would have had money to help me through treatment.
3. Share with those who are **ready** to receive information and have conversations or engage in resources about the subject matter. For example, listen to podcasts and thought leaders.

    This does not mean you have to share with the world because not everyone wants to hear that you're getting it together, but you may have a few people with whom you want to ride with you to the top.

This is just a suggestion, but it empowered me, solidified my understanding, and made me feel good about sharing the knowledge I learned. We're not here to hoard knowledge, but we also don't need to burden ourselves with people who aren't ready and will discourage us from making the necessary changes in our life.

4. Ask yourself, "What am I most excited to learn?" The world of personal finance is vast. While it seems overwhelming, there could be spaces where you will excel. Figure out what they are and empower yourself to explore the possibilities.

CHAPTER 3:

CAREER ALIGNMENT

"Your comfort zone isn't comfortable. It's familiar."
—Tiana Pollari

Are you doing what you want to do? Are you doing what you love to do? What's the next step in your career? What do you have to do to get there? Is it time for a complete change? Is there a hobby that you want to turn into a business? What are those things?

I always knew from an early age that I wanted to be a psychologist or lawyer. Actually, let's go back; initially, I wanted to be a farmer for reasons unknown because I grew up in the city. However, after that, I wanted to be a psychologist or lawyer. In my last year of high school, I had to decide, and I chose to pursue psychology in university. My goal was to be a psychologist or a professor, which meant I was going all the way for my PhD. When I graduated, I landed my first salaried position, making decent money by everyone else's account. I didn't pursue my master's degree right away. I remember my grandmother was so worried that I would get caught up and not finish school, but I wasn't blinded. I knew I wanted more. If I stayed, that would be my ceiling; there's no

Chapter 3: Career Alignment

way I could do this for the rest of my life. Hence, I took a leap and left to go to the United Kingdom to get my master's degree. When I was in the United Kingdom, I loved it. I had the best time and met wonderful friends that I still speak to today. Although I would have loved to stay to get my PhD, the British pound was relatively high in comparison to the Canadian dollar. I didn't want that burden on my mom, and I was out of options.

When I returned home, I landed a career in law enforcement. It seemed like an interesting transition for me, but I said I would love to learn about this population from a frontline perspective and then move on to be a forensic psychologist. I worked in law enforcement for about five years, and it was the most interesting experience that I have had. Besides the less-than-desirable things I saw, heard, and dealt with, I had the most beautiful friendships and made beautiful bonds with my partners, and it is something that I don't think I'll ever experience again at a workplace.

When I was diagnosed with cancer, I received an overwhelming amount of support. They called themselves #hansonsarmy, and they made bracelets and everything. This was then extended to friends from high school who I had no clue still cared about me. If any of you are reading this, thank you from the bottom of my heart. I don't know how I could express my love for you all. When I was off work, I missed my people. Although I did not miss being in an institution of any kind or the challenging environment that can come with working in law enforcement. I knew I missed the people, the ones who cared for me and the ones who looked out for me day in and day out. It was never my intention to work there forever, but it's easy to stay in places that you know you've outgrown due to the connections or the potential for higher earnings, however I knew it no longer aligned with what I wanted to do or who I was.

It was time to transition, and I had to commit to my transition during my medical leave. This was obviously a challenge because of what I was going through, but I had to prepare for where I wanted to stand when it was over. This was a whole new world, but I felt the misalignment with my career title and who I was more and more when entering social and professional spaces. I felt like I wasn't showing up as myself because I would have to create a story, so I wouldn't get into long, drawn-out details and stories about what my career entailed, what they saw on television, and what actually happened. For many people, their careers are tied to their identity. It takes up a lot of mental space to think about what you could do or be, which is why I think your career is so attached to your peace. It allows you to present yourself confidently when you're interacting with others. Unfortunately, at least in North America, I have noticed that the first things people ask are, "How are you? What do you do?" Your responses to those questions almost determine how they will treat you and how long they will engage with you.

My current career felt limiting, and I felt like I couldn't express myself fully. I had to hide parts of me and could not do simple things like networking engagements with a business card. This isn't to say other people can't or couldn't do it, but I had other plans in mind for myself. Despite loving my partners and the connections I had made, my job wasn't bringing me peace, and I could not imagine putting myself in that environment again, not even for a short while.

Chapter 3: Career Alignment

> *Visit peaceandsuccess.com to access this free resource:*
> *Career Satisfaction Tracker*

I remember having to put aside the negative talk that I heard such as, "When you work here, no one will want you," "You'll never get another job," "You'll never get another job that pays this much," or "You're damaged goods." None of this ever was directed at me because I never talked about my goals and dreams, but I heard it, and it passed through my mind. I had to put all that aside, drown out the noise, and commit to changing the narrative.

I couldn't let what I was hearing, what their opinions were, or what their limiting beliefs were derail me from what I wanted for myself. I knew what was good for me and what would align for me, and it wasn't this, and it wasn't here. Similarly, you must know where you are in your career and understand how it affects you because no one else will, and quite frankly, no one else cares. People operate from their experience and limitations; hence, asking them to see your dreams may be impossible because they can't even see their own dreams.

I will close this chapter with the following advice. Don't get caught up in other people's ideas of what is possible or don't stand in your own way because you're familiar with where you are. Take a leap of faith and commit to yourself. Commit to yourself for your peace of mind.

Take a moment to reflect on your own career.

Reflections

1. Evaluate where you are in your career and where you want to be.
2. Identify what is no longer serving you and what you would like more of in your career.
3. Determine the steps to get where you want to go.
4. How can you drown out the noise and commit to action?

PART TWO
MENTAL WELL-BEING

CHAPTER 4:

ALLOW YOURSELF IN

"Self-reflection entails asking yourself questions about your values, assessing your strengths and failures, thinking about your perceptions and interactions with others, and imagining where you want to take your life in the future."
—Robert L Rosen.

How well do you know yourself? Do you take time to understand your emotions when they come up? What do you do for yourself daily and weekly to nourish your soul? What rejuvenates you in your daily life? What depletes you?

If self-reflection was easy, everyone would do it, but it's not. In my experience, this is one of the most important areas of our lives and one of the most challenging things to do. I'm writing this book post-pandemic, which means I've seen so many people struggle to face themselves every day. Before the pandemic, we could run around, stay busy, go to restaurants, hang out with friends, go to nightclubs, and do all these things that distracted us and allowed us to avoid having real moments with ourselves. The pandemic changed a lot of that for many people. The pandemic forced us to face our unresolved issues or what some call our demons. They followed us everywhere, to the kitchen, to the bathroom, and to the bedroom. There was no escaping them. That may be a part of why many people broke down. We experienced loss, fear, and isolation, and we no longer had our usual outlets, which made it almost too much to bear. My heart was heavy to see the world navigate this challenging and polarizing time, but there was a sliver of light in those moments of triumph. Some people, including myself, were able to get a hold of the things that ate them up on the inside and held them back for years, and they were able to free themselves from them. I am grateful I made it through, and I want to take a second to send love to those who have lost loved ones and still are managing the effects of their loss.

My experience taught me that learning to understand yourself and figuring out what makes you tick allows you to see life differently, and it makes it significantly more enjoyable because you are aligning with your own needs. However, the reality is that it's hard. It takes time, and quite frankly, it takes a great amount of will to be honest with yourself. In addition, we all have what I like to call our default thoughts and emotions, which are the ones we received, learned, and observed from the world around us—things we learned along the way from our family and friends. Left untamed, if we never stop to question these default thoughts or emotions, we may continue to hold them with no understanding about why we are doing it. For me, I watched my mom be a boss and independent woman. She got things done, never with a tear in her eye and never allowing anyone to walk all over her. This translated into me hiding many emotions and believing others would not or could not show up for me in the way I needed.

Chapter 4: Allow Yourself In

I learned that you must be self-reliant and independent because people are unreliable, and it's easier to do it yourself. This perspective seemingly has its benefits, and it buffers you from disappointment and feeds the ego from doing it all on your own. However, it does you a disservice because you may not be able to let people in, and you are subject to burnout. Hiding your emotions does not mean they are not there; you have just shifted them to another time. While I had been journalling from an early age, I didn't really understand why I was doing it, so there would be points when I would stop writing, and in its place, I developed this unhealthy bottle system. I would just hold my emotions in and keep them together until the bottle filled up. Then, I would cry uncontrollably to myself about everything up to that point, which would reset the bottle. I remember once, my mom and I were talking about something fairly emotionally charged. I don't remember the details of the conversation, but once one tear started forming, we left one another and went to our rooms to cry alone. It took me reflecting on those moments to understand why I was operating like that, and I had to process and how my emotional bottle was not serving me. It was challenging because this is what I knew and what I saw, and this was my normal.

> *Visit peaceandsuccess.com to access this free resource:*
> *Your Default Story Worksheet*

My mother provided me with a solid foundation, I was confident, and I felt that I could navigate this world on my own. I leaned into myself more than I sought comfort from others. I was a person to whom people came for comfort; maybe it was because I was an only child with siblings from my father's side who I only saw on weekends. Perhaps it allowed me to take the time to sit by myself. Maybe it was just who I was. I'm not really sure, but I was able to communicate my needs, but I was not able to express my emotions consistently. My mom always told me that from an early age, I knew exactly what I liked and didn't like, and I would articulate it. Some called me stubborn, and they may be right, but I also think that it helped me a great deal. I also believe that it is critical to take the time to understand yourself in order to communicate your needs with confidence and assertiveness. I understand that assertiveness can make people uncomfortable because they believe it makes them appear mean or rude, but assertiveness, in my opinion, creates boundaries, and boundaries pave the way for respect.

It took me a long time to understand how this relationship with myself helped me navigate through one of the most challenging times in my life. The day I was diagnosed with cancer, somehow, I didn't self-destruct. I knew something was wrong, but the doctor didn't believe me. I had gone to the hospital three times that week, and they wanted to send me home with an antacid (that I could have bought over the counter at any local drug store). The third time I went in, I had to advocate for myself, and I let them know I was not leaving, and I would wait for as long as it took to get a scan. Unfortunately, being a young woman of color does not earn you the benefit of the doubt that your pain is real. When the results came in, the emergency doctor knew immediately that it was most likely cancer, and I was admitted right away. In my heart of hearts, I already knew something was wrong. This was just the confirmation.

Chapter 4: Allow Yourself In

The next moments felt surreal. I let him finish explaining the course of action. I was finally able to invite my partner in, so he could ask questions, and then it began. This was a real thing that was happening, and I had to let my loved ones know, so I took my time, took a breath, and called my family and friends individually. Looking back, I was so calm, as though I was calling to make dinner plans. I remember standing in the waiting room, making each call, and looking at the news playing on the television. Many of them didn't even know how to react because I wasn't reacting. I was just stating the facts, and at no point was I hysterical or even crying. I remember calling my sister, and she said, "I'm in disbelief, but I don't even know what to do because you don't sound concerned." I guess a part of me never was. Although I knew that I was facing my own mortality, it felt like just another unfortunate thing that was happening. I didn't know why it was happening, but I intended to move through it even if the outcome was unknown.

The only thing I knew was that I had to believe that I had everything I needed to fight, and if I got caught up in crying, I'd be too exhausted to show up for myself. It would be a downward spiral that would be exceedingly difficult to break, so I chose peace in a time of chaos. I wasn't trying to think positively, this was not the time for that. I had cancer, and sure, I was alive, but c'mon. I had stage four cancer just like that? That is not a positive situation. It was just what it was, and it was something I had to experience. I had people tell me, "You are going to be fine," but that's just something people say. They would say, "You won't lose your hair; a lot of people don't." I can assure you I definitely lost all of my hair, but I was prepared for it.

I started cutting my hair off before treatment, so the effect was less dramatic. I read research studies on what the effects would be, what to expect for my type of cancer, and what recovery was like. Some said I shouldn't read up on it because that only would make it worse, but I wanted to know. If the plan was for me to leave this Earth, I knew I was leaving whether I read the article or not, but at least I was informed. However, my perspective reflected that I knew what worked for me and what brought me peace, and not knowing or educating myself would keep me up at night. Listening to everyone else's advice about what I should do and how I should do it for a unique individual experience such as this would not serve me, but I had to recognize that.

Knowing who you are and how you navigate your emotions equips you with the tools you need to get through hardships because you have the energy and resources to focus on the present, and you know exactly what you need to do. It brings you peace knowing that you have a system, and whatever is on the other side of this challenge has to work out the way it's intended. For me, that may not have been life or coming out physically whole, and I would have had to deal with that. What I can say is each cancer experience is different and unique, and I cannot and will not speak for everyone. I don't know how I'm here or why I survived when many others just as deserving of life didn't, but I know it is a blessing to be here because we don't all make it.

I want to send love to all those who have lost someone and those who are still here and are fighting to stay. My heart is with you. This speaks to more than cancer because we all have experiences, and we must undergo challenges. We do not all process these events the same way, but knowing how you process them, what you need, and how to maintain your peace in the chaos is important. This allows you to move through it and avoid getting stuck in the mud but move like the tide. Eventually, things will calm, and you can carry on.

I know the wellness industry has been marketed quite heavily. Things like mindfulness, yoga, and meditation sometimes seem out of reach, "hippie," or don't reflect an inclusive lifestyle. I don't dispute your feelings or how things seem; however, I can say we all need wellness practices, and in my opinion, it shouldn't be optional. It's important to understand who we are, take an emotional inventory, and examine our perspectives and the ways we process the world. I like to journal because it gives me clarity, and it is a great tool for releasing thoughts and goal setting. I also do intentional walks where I don't listen to music. I just think of possibilities, things on my mind, and my goals and aspirations. It's unbelievable how much you have running through your mind and how quickly you forget that there hasn't been any music playing. Journaling or walking does not have to be your thing, but you should have a thing. If you don't yet, that's okay; just take the time to explore what it may be.

Reflecting allows you the possibility to make space for peace. Reflecting allows you to understand how you navigate the world, and it can give insight into how the world receives you and treats you. Do people tend to walk all over you while they treat others with respect? Do they celebrate you and love you for who you are? What are those positive qualities and areas you can modify or nurture? As we grow through life, we are always changing and evolving, and it is through self-reflection that we are able to see just how that change is serving us. In understanding yourself, you become less shaken by the outside world, and you can navigate the world with internal peace and truly be all you want to be.

Take the time to know yourself and understand how you process the world.

Reflections

1. What are your default perceptions? Do you tend to perceive things negatively or positively throughout your day?
2. Do you have the ability to remain neutral and not attach meaning to every instance?
3. How do you deal with a challenge? Are you able to overcome a negative moment, or does it ruin your day or week?
4. How do you cultivate joy in your day?
5. What is your greatest quality? How do you show up for yourself? How would you like to show up for yourself?

If these questions seem beyond you or evoke emotions, please reach out to someone you trust or explore available resources on mental health online or in person. I cannot give you a whole list because I don't know where you are in the world and what your access to resources are. However, I hope this information is helpful and can lead you to find ways to support yourself and identify external support.

CHAPTER 5:

HIGHER POWER

"I believe in God and a higher power. I'm still not a religious type per se because religion tore my family apart. I'm still a little scared and skeptical of being the one with any faith."
—Jeffrey Atkins.

What role does faith play in your life? How do you connect to something greater than you? How does faith impact your present or future? Do you consider yourself to be religious, and what does that mean to you?

I'm sure with whatever I'm going to say, someone may take offense simply because we're talking about religion, faith, and spirituality. I ask that in this chapter, you take what you need and leave what you don't. Please understand that all I share is through my lens and my experience, and it is not intended to hurt or offend anyone in their experience or faith.

Let's begin. I grew up Christian and later learned that it was Pentecostal although I didn't know much about what that meant. I knew I went to church on the church bus on Sundays with my mom. I went to Sunday school and gave my weekly offering with a dollar left for an after-church Jamaican patty. I was in the children's choir, and we went on church trips like Darien Lake. I enjoyed it. It was fun. Then, I got older and started asking questions. At that point, it was no longer just about fun, as I wondered, *"What's happening here?"* I was beginning to understand the stories of the Bible and the culture dynamic of the church a little bit more, and things were not adding up for me (and not because I wasn't good at math). I had questions. I always have been very inquisitive, and I like to understand things in their entirety. To my surprise, asking questions about God and church was not really welcomed, or maybe they did not welcome the type of questions I was asking.

There was one situation when I was with an elder, speaking to the pastor, who was talking about the evolution of times and things that were acceptable and not acceptable in today's world. He said that boring or piercing your ears now was acceptable and it was okay for women to have piercings because the times had evolved. Then, I asked about tattoos, and he abruptly said people shouldn't have tattoos. Confused, I mentioned that a lot of people have tattoos now, even spiritual, or cultural ones, and I asked why tattoos weren't part of the time. He was firm on his stance, and he said people should not have tattoos. At that moment, I realized this was a man—respectfully. He was a man who was determining what we could and could not do although it conflicted with what I read in the Bible. I wondered, *are we doing as the Bible says or as man says?* I was perplexed, and I started to lose a bit of my faith because I felt like they were picking and choosing what could or couldn't be done. Perhaps, I had the wrong idea and the wrong view of what that meant, but at that moment, it felt as though

Chapter 5: Higher Power

we were selecting what we could and could not do based on who was at the head of the church.

As I got older, I tried to find my own church—my place to figure things out. I knew I believed in and was still connected with God, but I was finding it challenging in the church. I thought I finally found a church I liked until I noticed little things like people passing judgment (God does not need our help) or leaders of the church saying things I did not agree with. If I'm being honest and probably very controversial, I didn't love it when people dictated or berated how someone should love or who they could love. It seemed conflicting again because I felt that they were saying, "God loves all people, but not you or you." That never sat right with me. I guess I should say that I don't even have any tattoos, and I'm in a happy heterosexual relationship, but that doesn't matter to me. What matters is that we should be acting out of love, and what we should be saying and doing should be the reflection of God and not a reflection of man.

I began asking less of others, and I sought to understand on my own. I started exploring and reading about other faiths. Through this exploration, I found philosophies that actually allowed me to understand my God more. I didn't talk about it to others because I didn't want anyone to say, "Oh no, we have to save her." I didn't need to be saved. I wanted to understand; I wanted to understand my God. By exploring other religions and other faiths, I understood how that relationship should look. I understood that we are images of God. God is working through us, and we are to reflect God. Maybe, I didn't have a problem with God, and maybe my issue was more with the church. Therefore, in my humble opinion, exploration, for me, wasn't rejection.

It's okay to seek clarity to augment or modify your belief system. Sometimes, we grow up with a belief system, the default system, which might not be in alignment with what we actually believe, and it's okay to take the time to explore that and find something that aligns with you and who you are.

> *Visit peaceandsuccess.com to access this free resource:*
> *A Moment of Faith Journal Prompt*

When I was diagnosed with cancer, I can tell you that my faith wavered in all kinds of directions. I couldn't understand it. As much as I was trying to navigate in the light, it seemed like there was so much darkness around me. As I said, it became quite comical. My whole journey felt like I was a fly on the wall while I watched the story unfold. I couldn't make sense of God at that moment because misfortune was putting some work in. My mom was paralyzed, and there was nothing I could do to change it. My great-uncle was hospitalized for months after being hit by a tractor trailer. I lost my childhood friend, and I underwent the deepest grief I have ever felt (may your soul rest in peace Mark), and now I was diagnosed with cancer. I was trying to be the best person I could be and show up for myself and others while I continued to experience this hardship.

However, I had to sit with that – all of it. Why would I be immune to hardship? Who said you don't experience pain or challenge if you're a "good" person? Who said there's a limit to the hardships we experience? These things were undesirable, and what was happening to me was unbelievable. I felt pain, disbelief, and sadness, but I didn't suffer. I was not suffering. I was moving through these emotions as I put my faith in God, and I felt that what was going to would be. I also sat with something else that I got from my spiritual exploration. Maybe none of this is even about me. Maybe it's what can be done through me, and I had to take the time to unpack that. I had the tools to deal with this, so why not me? I would much rather it be me than anyone I love, and maybe He knew that.

I also don't think of it as one of those statements that we tell others such as, "God gives His toughest battles to his strongest soldiers" (or maybe I am in denial) because I can assure you that I am tired of being on this battlefield and ready to lay down. Perhaps, I just had to be the one. So even though my faith was wavering, I talked to God about it, and He understood that respectfully, I just needed time. I still don't think I needed to have cancer to be enlightened because I was already on my way, and I don't know that I ever will see it as a gift, but maybe it was just a thing that happened that tested every part of my being, and I can be at peace if it had to be me and not a loved one.

Present-day, God and I are good. Although I still don't go to church, we have long conversations, and I pray several times a day. At this stage in my life, going to church does not align with me, and it brings me more discomfort than it does peace. What I can say is this. Your faith is your own, and sometimes, it presents challenges. For me, believing in something greater than yourself can give you hope, courage, and peace of mind. There's always something else at play, and we don't always know what. I know the saying is, "Everything happens for a reason," but when it's intertwined with trauma and hardship, we can spend a lot of time trying to find out what the reason is and why we deserve it. I think it's more important to find ways to move through the challenges and build your toolkit because this life is not easy, and unfortunately, I don't think there's someone out there with a flip chart equally distributing misfortune.

Faith is challenging, and I'm not going to be the one to tell you to believe in one thing or another, but I do think that we should connect to something outside ourselves as well as connect to ourselves. We need something to give us hope, that there is more to the world than just us, even if we can't see it. We can hope that something out there is enriching our lives, so we can hold on to small signs of joy, express gratitude, and experience peace of mind.

Take the time to reflect on what works for you. Identify what spiritual practices can ground you and prepare you for your days. I wake up in the mornings, sit on the edge of my bed, and say a gratitude prayer. I get myself ready and head out for a morning walk. This brings me so much clarity, allows me to explore my thoughts, and sets the tone for the day. When I return, I light a candle or use my clay diffuser with some essential oils. There's nothing like coming out of the shower to your favorite scents. I have discovered that my mornings are an important part of my day; it is the time I hold dear to myself. Sometimes, things happen, or winter happens, and I have to change the routine, but what remains a constant, is taking the time for myself, connecting to my faith, and practices that ground me.

Take a moment to reflect on the role of faith in your life.

Reflections

1. Evaluate the role of faith in your life.
2. What are the questions that you have about your current faith? Have you taken the time to explore them?
3. What gives you hope for a brighter tomorrow?
4. How do you connect with what gives you hope? How often?
5. What are the rituals that you do to nurture that connection when you are feeling low or when you are happy?

PART THREE
INTERCONNECTIONS

CHAPTER 6:

KNOW YOUR PRESENCE

"The better you know yourself,
the better your relationship with the world."
—Toni Collete.

Have you ever taken the time to listen and reflect on how you make people feel? Do people love being around you? Do they only bring gossip and negativity to you? Do they bring their best moments and their best days to you?

Who I am has been relatively clear for a long time, which came from a lot of reflection and understanding of how I didn't want to be and how I would like to show up for others and myself. I've often been described as optimistic, loving, kind, supportive, dependable, and rational. However, I also know I can be super sarcastic, stubborn, extremely reserved, matter of fact, and I am quickly turned off by lying and inconsistency. Being the eldest of my siblings on my dad's side and an only child for my mother made me quite responsible; I learned from my mistakes rather quickly, and I adopted a strong moral compass at a young age. However, I also took the time to acknowledge what was on the other side. I noticed that sometimes people would shy away from telling me things because of who I was, and I didn't understand it. I felt like I was always supportive and wanted the best for those around me, but then I realized that maybe that was the problem. Maybe the definition of what's best differs for people, and it is contextual. Maybe not everyone wants, is ready for, or feel they deserve the best for themselves.

Someone I love and trust was able to break it down to me like this. Because I'm so clear on my boundaries—what I want and don't want—it can feel hard to share with me or mess up when you're still trying to figure things out yourself. I found this super interesting because in my head, while I'm clear on my boundaries, I still see myself as someone who also is figuring things out, and where I am is just what is working for me at this moment. I remember a high school friend telling me she would hide things from me because she didn't want me to be mad at her or disappointed. Another person close to me told me that I process information quickly and logically, and not everyone comes to logic as quickly as I do, which can be challenging for the other person.

Apparently, I was giving off mom vibes, that I had it all together, and my ability to arrive at logical conclusions quickly sometimes made people question themselves. I realized that my navigation system sometimes can create a challenge for people because they feel like they have to live up to it. However, in my mind, I was just figuring it all out and actively trying to make sense of the world and myself. My desire was and is to love and support those around me. My intention is never to determine how they should live their lives. Therefore, I learned that while it can be hard, it's important to be open to receiving feedback and reflecting on that feedback or observations. While your intentions may be good, they may not be received in that same way. We are experiencing information based on our lens and level of understanding. No one is perfect, and seemingly good qualities have implications on interactions and the way people view you.

> *Visit peaceandsuccess.com to access this free resource:*
> *Receiving Feedback Tips*

When I was diagnosed with cancer, I also realized that how I navigated the world had consequences. It made some people uncomfortable, and they didn't know what to do or say about it. Some felt they didn't know how to be sad because I didn't appear sad. Some shied away because they were sad and couldn't deal with seeing me in an ill state or picture life without me. Even then, I had to understand how my perceived strength played a role in how others received my situation. I read about how family and friends can experience the diagnoses of their loved ones. I tried to make space for people to ask questions and clarify anything that may have been confusing. I reached out to friends I knew were having a tough time and made space for them to express themselves. I remember seeing the look in my nephew's eyes, not knowing what was happening but knowing that something wasn't okay with me. I had to find the words to explain what was going on. I read about how family and friends can experience the diagnoses of their loved ones.

You may think I shouldn't have to try to understand others during something like cancer, and maybe that's what works for other people, but I know that cancer didn't just affect me. It affected everyone who loved and cared about me, so I did what I had the capacity to do. While I didn't want to spend my days consoling others about my diagnoses, I felt if there were questions, I could answer them to give my loved one's peace of mind. I could handle that. Knowing yourself allows you to understand how you relate to others, how to support them when they need, and how they can support you in your time of need. It allows for more pleasant and fulfilling interactions for both parties. While my confidence and grounded demeanor may come off as though I've got it all figured out, I can assure you I do not. I see myself on an evolving journey where I am open to learning every step of the way.

Take a moment to reflect on how you relate to others.

Reflections

1. How do you impact the spaces you enter?
2. How do you feel in social situations? Do you feel energized? Do you feel depleted?
3. How do your friends and family describe you? Are there any characteristics you would like to work on?
4. What is the quality that people love about you? How does it impact your relationships?
5. What qualities do you value and love about yourself?

CHAPTER 7:

FRIENDS AND FAMILY

"I will not allow anyone to walk in my mind with dirty feet."
—Gandhi.

When was the last time you evaluated the relationships in your life? Do you have legacy friendships that are no longer serving you? Are there individuals who make you feel bad about yourself or drain your energy? Are their family members who have zero boundaries when it comes to you and only you?

Growing up, I was a genuinely nice person, and I noticed that sometimes, people would take advantage of that or mostly just be ungrateful. I found myself always trying to understand, well, *why would they do that? I'm so nice to them.* I didn't understand that people are operating only from their lens. I realized that I gave a lot in my friendships. I tried to be there. I tried to be kind, and I tried to include everyone, but I noticed that I kept getting the short end of the stick. As I grew up, I learned that I had to modify my friendships. I liked who I was, but I didn't like how certain people made me feel. I learned that I could be kind, but I didn't always have to be nice. Instead of changing who I was, I changed the people whom I was around and the number of people I allowed to be close to me.

This, for me, is not only exclusive to friendships, as it most certainly includes family. Family can be the most beautiful and supportive network in your life, but family also can be frustrating, and they can hurt you in ways you never imagined. This is a harsh reality I learned growing up. I won't get into the particulars because we all have a story about a family member or family members who drain us and take from us. We wish they were better, and every single time, they disappoint us.

This can be extremely challenging to navigate because our family can be wrapped up in our core being. They impact how we feel about ourselves and how we understand the world. I had to go to therapy for it because I couldn't move past it on my own; it kept coming up in unwanted places. It was taking up far too much mental space; it was holding me back. It's important to understand how relationships impact you and what you need to do for yourself to alleviate this impact. Sometimes, we need to do an inventory and evaluate our relationships based on our values and needs. It's okay to outgrow people. It's okay to assert yourself, and it's okay to distance yourself from people who no longer are serving you. This, for me, is a crucial factor because your family and friends can bring you the most joy, but quite frankly, they can break you and leave you in the deepest darkest places. I took the time to evaluate my friends and family, and I'm so happy that I did.

> *Visit peaceandsuccess.com to access this free resource:*
> *Friends and Family Inventory*

Chapter 7: Friends and Family

When I was going through treatment, so many people showed up for me, and I received an overwhelming amount of love and support. Still, on the other side, so many people didn't show up for me. Many of these people were family members from whom I did not hear a word from. I thought it would hurt more, but it just confirmed what I already knew. It's not necessary to hold on to familial relationships just because you "should" if they make you question yourself or disrupt your peace of mind. I can assure you I did take time to look at it from all angles, and I accounted for the fact that people struggle with mortality and seeing others sick; however, from my observation, a lot of what happened was a choice. It is honestly okay, and I do not say this sarcastically or bitterly because when you experience deep grief and illness, what becomes clearer is whether you lived to tell the tale or not, the Earth would continue to revolve around the sun. Therefore, I send love from the greatest of distances, and I choose never to be disgruntled by other people having their own experiences in this life.

Cancer can be a lonely journey because no one else knows what you're going through. No one else feels what you feel. They want to be there, but they don't know what the right things are to say, and they end up saying things that don't necessarily resonate with you like, "I knew a friend of a friend who drank grape juice and was cured." Still, I never ever felt like I wasn't supported. I had kept such good people in my life, and they showed up for me when it counted, even though I hardly ever went to any of them for help. I realized that I was able to attract the right people and keep the right people in my life who showed up for me when I was in need. If I only had kept people in my life who depleted me, angered me, and just wanted to load their problems on me, I would have felt alone during that time of my life. I would have been exhausted and would have felt like my friends didn't love me for me but for what I could do for them. Instead, I was wrapped in the biggest blanket of love imaginable for which I forever will be grateful.

Evaluating your friendships protects your peace, and that allows you to be supported when you need it. I think about it now, as I'm writing this book and changing the trajectory of my life, how all these people showed up for me, and all I had to do was ask for help (which I also had to learn to do). All I had to do was say, "Hey, would you be able to help me with this?" and people came together in their own unique way to support me in getting this book done.

Prioritizing ourselves can be challenging, especially when it comes to family. I found this particularly difficult when I became a full-time caregiver to my mother when she became paralyzed. I felt like I was juggling a million things, roles, and responsibilities. I felt like a parent, a child, a nurse, and everything in between, depending on the moment. There were times when I wasn't doing what I needed for myself, or I was not doing enough of it, and I would be completely drained. This is when resentment towards the situation would build up. I knew I wasn't mad at her because neither of us asked for this tragic thing she was experiencing. I had to learn that it was okay to tell her I needed time for myself and spend as much time as needed alone. I had to learn to be okay saying no to sitting and watching tv with her because I needed a moment. I had to learn not to take on the guilt of not being around all the time or being frustrated about the situation.

Family pushes you in ways that a lot of other people cannot. I've learned that it might not always be the most peaceful course to remove certain people from your life completely, especially your family members who are around a lot. What I also learned was I can modify the access that they have to me, physically and mentally, and by that, I mean I can change the level of interaction I have with them. I can change how long we speak, when we speak, and how frequently we see each other. Through these modifications, I gain some control over the situation, and I'm able to maintain my peace of mind by not engaging in disruptive conversations.

Take a moment to reflect on your relationships.

Reflections

1. How do people in your life make you feel? Make a list of your family and friends.
2. How can you modify or remove those people who are depleting you from your life?
3. How does support from your family and friends look to you?
4. How do you honor those who show up for you and bring you joy? This is important to me because it's great if your family and friends are showing up for you, but how are you honoring them?

Too often, we forget to give people the love and respect they deserve when they show up for us time and time again. Take the time to tell people that you love them. Take the time to buy your friends flowers and show people how you can support them. Ask your family members or friends what they need. I think that is very important. Don't assume what your friends need from you because that's how you receive love, or that's what you need.

CHAPTER 8:

ROMANTIC RELATIONSHIPS

"Genuine relationships depend first on a healthy relationship with ourselves" — Sonia Choquette

Do you know what your needs are in a relationship? If you are in a relationship, why are you in a relationship with that person? How does it make you feel? How do you show up in relationships? Do you understand your worth, and are you able to articulate it? Does your partner know themselves and treat you with respect? How do you want to be loved?

What I find fascinating is how quickly who we are and how we show up for ourselves can change when we are in a romantic relationship. You can know what you want and articulate it with clarity, and you still can end up with someone who is the exact opposite of what you desire. I don't know the science behind it, but love has a powerful influence over our decisions, and sometimes, it voids all logic. I was single for three years before I met my partner, and I can assure you I was not looking. I was living what I thought was, you know, my best life. I was enjoying my time with my friends, traveling, and enjoying time with myself, and overall, just having an enjoyable time.

Chapter 8: Romantic Relationships

Sometimes, I had people tell me that I should be dating or trying to find someone because I was getting older. I heard shocking things like I shouldn't be so particular because I should be having kids by now. They essentially were telling me I should settle. That, for me, was obviously laughable. I wasn't worried about any of that. I knew when the time was right, I would find someone who respected and loved me, and it wouldn't be a matter of just having to find someone for the sake of having someone, which unfortunately, is the pressure that women often experience in society. This can lead us to end up with partners who aren't ready for relationships, or we end up with partners who aren't giving us what we need. Because we haven't defined our boundaries clearly, or we don't know our worth, our partners question it or take advantage of our vulnerability.

When I met my partner, I already knew what I wanted. I learned from past experiences the things that didn't work for me and things that I desired. At one point, I thought I was emotionally closed off. That I am not really the hand holding type, and I do not want to talk or see someone all the time. I can assure you I am not that. I want all the love. I want someone to spend quality time with me, hold me, and show up for me. It's funny how we adapt to situations that may conflict entirely with what we want and desire. Maybe we do it to keep the person we are with who we know can't give us what we want, or in my case, we are young and haven't quite figured out how we want to be loved. Whatever it is, I think understanding what you want, and need can allow you to determine what kind of partner is best for you rather than trying to change someone into the person you want.

On my first date with my partner, I knew how I wanted to be treated. I knew how I wanted to feel, and more importantly, I could articulate it. He asked questions that I was able to answer clearly and plainly. On our second date, I remember we talked about character, values, and expectations, so in the event that either of us wanted to leave, that would have been the appropriate time. However, we have been together ever since and there is so much love here. In our relationship, what I always found comforting is knowing that if he or I walked away, I would be fine, not because I don't love him with all my heart, but because I've cultivated a strong sense of self-worth. Our relationship is built on mutual respect and understanding, and we both recognize that our individual well-being is crucial for the health of our partnership. This foundation of self-assurance allows us to love and support each other without dependency, fostering a connection that thrives on our shared values and personal growth. I will never claim that it's perfect, but I can say that it's beautiful.

My worth is not and has never been wrapped up in whether I was in a relationship, no matter how people try to put that on women. I understand there is sometimes the intersection of cultural pressures and family telling you that you aren't good enough because you haven't found someone, or maybe you have the wrong someone. What I can say is love yourself. Show up for yourself. We can't control the wild things people feel it's appropriate to say to women about their appearance and bodies, but please love yourself as you are right here and right now. The ability to do so gives you so much power, confidence, and the ability to walk in a room with your head high. Sometimes, I walk into rooms feeling so good and thinking everyone is admiring me. Then, I actually look around, and absolutely no one is looking at me and people are just minding their business; I laugh and carry on. Surely, they were looking at me at some point, right? However, I say all that to say, how you love yourself will determine how someone can and will love you. Leave no room, and I repeat, no room for other people to determine your worth and how they are going to treat you.

Chapter 8: Romantic Relationships

> *Visit peaceandsuccess.com to access this free resource:*
> *Defining Your Love Worksheet*

It was the middle of 2019, and I was in a relationship where we connected on many levels. The first time he met my mom, she was in a hospital bed, and we were three months into our relationship. We had conversations about how my life would change, and I told him he was free to go live his life, but that was where my focus was going to be. He chose to stay because he loved what we had, and he wanted to support me. Despite all that was going on, there was peace in my relationship, and I was grateful for that safe place. Little did I know that I would be diagnosed with cancer a year later. I felt bad because of these dramatic life events that I kept bringing to him, and part of me blamed myself. Again, I told him he didn't have to stay for this, and he looked at me strangely, and he told me he was not going anywhere.

People always told me I was lucky he stayed, which always gave me mixed emotions. Even though I gave him an option, it felt like they were saying I wasn't worth a thing now because of my diagnosis. I doubted my worth for a brief moment, thinking who would love me after cancer, but I caught myself on the way down. With or without cancer, I am worth it; I am the rarest gift, and I am the last one of me anyone will find. When I came to my senses, I realized I just didn't want to burden anyone or put anyone through the series of unfortunate events about to be my life, not because I suddenly was tarnished. However, to my disbelief, I learned that disregarding the unwell is very much a thing. I read stories about how people had their best friends or spouses leave them, and they just completely disappeared. I was shocked because I never could imagine doing that, but I guess there are levels to what people can handle.

This reinforced that if you don't know your worth, people have the opportunity to tell you what it is or project their issues onto you. I never wanted to feel like I was indebted and obligated to stay if something no longer was working in the relationship. It was more was important than ever that I did not lose sight of who I was despite what was happening.

During treatment, I still wanted to show up for my partner and support him in his endeavors. I navigated a new relationship as a full-time caregiver who was dealing with grief, cancer, and a global pandemic, and that took work. We had to make decisions on reproductive options, and he watched me change physically and emotionally. He was not only giving me buzzcuts, but we were also receiving brochures about the impact of cancer on intimacy. Not exactly romantic. Needless to say, a lot happened fast, not to mention the challenges or responsibilities taking place in his world.

Having the right conversations and the right person beside you is important. Both parties have to be willing to learn, grow, and communicate. I think I also should add that both parties have to learn to be vulnerable. My partner is a kind, gentle soul, and I am so unbelievably grateful for his love and continued support. The more you connect with another person, the clearer it becomes that we are all navigating the world from our life experiences; we may have traumas, triggers, and stories that shaped us. Understanding how you both have dealt with or will deal with these things is important to supporting and connecting with your partner. Had I chosen someone who did not align with my values and didn't take the time to meet my needs, or had I failed to take the time to understand him, my experience would have been very different. We probably would not have made it. I probably would have been distracted and sad rather than using my energy and resources to heal. I would have been depleted, trying to maintain a relationship or heartbroken because it ended with me in a vulnerable place.

Love can be beautiful, but it also can hurt us and limit us mentally, financially, and professionally if we're not careful. It's important that we show up for ourselves, love ourselves, prioritize our peace, and choose our relationships wisely. We have to be in situations that make us feel good. We need to be in places that empower us to be the best versions of ourselves. Anything that doesn't make us feel good inside is not for us, and you have to define what that is. You know when your partner or friends aren't empowering you to be the best version of yourself. You know when they're taking from you—from your heart, soul, and peace of mind. Ask yourself, "What are my needs in a relationship? Are they being met? How often do I evaluate my needs?" This is something that I often do.

A friend of mine asked if I still evaluate my needs at this stage in my relationship. The answer was yes; I absolutely do because I have noticed that needs can change depending on where we are in our lives and what we are doing. As I take this time to write this book, what I need from my partner has changed, and I have to be able to articulate that rather than just expecting him to know (I had to work on that one). Now, I need him to support me differently. I love watching our shows together, but now I need time and space to get things done or even just to think. I also need him to listen, not always to solve a problem. Sometimes I just need him to be there as I process and commit to this journey. One of the most important things I want to note is some people don't know how to love you, nor do they desire to love you the way you want and deserve to be loved. I am here to tell you that you absolutely deserve the kind of love you want, but you have to define how it looks and meet it with supportive actions.

Take a moment to reflect on your romantic needs.

Reflections

1. Do you know what your needs are and how do you communicate them? Do you assume that your partner knows what you want?

2. What are your boundaries, and how do you respond when they're not respected? Do you just brush it off? If you communicate boundaries without enforcing them, you have suggestions, and people will overstep them all the time.

3. How do you show up for your partner in your relationship? Maybe you don't have a partner now, but how do you show up for the people who you are seeking a relationship with or how would you like to?

4. Do you know what your partner's needs are? Have you ever asked them how they want to be loved? How do they want to be cared for? We must acknowledge that how we want to be loved and how we define love may not always be the way someone receives love and defines love.

5. How do you want to be loved today? Reminder, you are never too much and deserve all the love that you desire.

PART FOUR
PHYSICAL HEALTH

CHAPTER 9:

PHYSICAL STORY

"I'm all about body positivity and self-love because
I believe that we can save the world if we first save ourselves."
—Melissa Jefferson

What is the story you tell yourself about your body? Whose body are you idolizing? What is on your list of New Year's resolutions to change? What parts of yourself do you absolutely love?

Growing up, there was never a point in my life when I was skinny. I always had meat on my body, I had an athletic build. This had its challenges when I was a little girl because sometimes, I either felt fat, I was called fat, or I didn't care about being a girl at all. I would wear pantsuits, oversized clothes, and athletic attire. As I got older, I would try to dabble in feminine clothing, but I hated my legs. I was allergic to mosquitos, and I got scared easily, so those trips to Jamaica had my legs looking like connect-the-dots. I would look around and see other people with zero scars, and here I was with all these mosquito bites and every scrape I got from playing outside. Not to mention, when I step on the scale, I'm heavier than everyone else with all these imperfections.

I was starting to not like my body. I don't know when it switched for me, but one day I remember wearing a skirt, feeling fantastic, and never looking back. Yes, I had scars, but I didn't care. I realized going on scales made me anxious, so I stopped going on them. To this day, I don't weigh myself. Even when I was going through chemotherapy, they weighed me at the beginning of every session, and I looked away every single time. I didn't need that negativity in my life. I have cancer, and I also am going to be preoccupied with my weight? No thanks. I struggled with acne later in life, and sometimes, I still do. I have tried many things including diet, exercise, topical treatments, and hormonal supplements, but unfortunately, it's one of those things that I can't shake. Your skin really can play on you emotionally, and that really is the only reason I started wearing makeup. It used to stress me out, which probably made it worse, but now, I just let it happen. My skin isn't perfect; many people don't have perfect skin or perfect anything, so I just choose to be kind to myself and ride it out. It eventually calms itself, and order is restored, so I do my best not to obsess about it.

> *Visit peaceandsuccess.com to access this free resource:*
> *Physical Story Worksheet*

Let me tell you though, this cool, calm, collected demeanor was put to the test when I had to shave my head. I remember people saying one of two things, "It's just hair" (please don't say that) and "You probably won't lose your hair; I heard of people who didn't" (that also is not helpful). There are many forms of cancer, and I had blood cancer, which requires a different treatment than solid tumor cancer, such as pancreatic cancer. Such treatment also varies in intensity based on the stage and location of the cancer, so it's hard to generalize and know what someone will experience based on an experience you may or may not have heard about. I know people were trying to comfort me, which is why I didn't lose sleep over their comments, but I also knew I had to prepare myself.

I had curly, dark, medium to long hair, and I didn't want to watch it fall out from that length. That, to me, seemed too dramatic, and it would be stressful to watch. So, I cut it in a short style, left a little on the top, and let it fall out from there. It definitely started falling out, clumps at a time. I was surprised I had any hair left the first time I saw it come out in my hands. Slowly, I cut more off until I watched a video of myself, and there were patches that I apparently hadn't seen. I was so embarrassed, and I just had to laugh to myself. I was shocked that I was walking around looking like that, thinking that I looked cute. That's when I went to the barber and just cut it all off. Some said I could have just shaved it from the beginning, but that's not what I wanted. This was something I could control, and I wanted to delay looking like a cancer patient for as long as I could, so I did. For some, buzzing it straight from the jump helps them; for me, I liked my cute short cut. I never had short hair before, so it was something different for a while, which brings me back to knowing what you need for your own contentment.

The world will have an unlimited number of opinions and ideas; knowing what you want and what works for and just doing that is extremely freeing, and it brings you so much peace. Did I ever think I would be bald? Nope. Did I ever think I would be cute and bald? Absolutely not, but I did what I could to be at peace with it.

When it comes to my appearance now, I am trying to find more ways to love myself. As I'm writing this, I'm looking at my post-cancer body, my post-COVID-19 body, and it's hard because I never looked like this. I don't know if visually it looks as dramatic as I feel, but I know that my body composition is different. I gain weight and build muscle differently. I have never seen my arms this size, nor have I ever put on a blazer in my closet that did not fit me. I'm learning this new body, which is sometimes hard, extremely hard. However, if I don't love it, who will? Rather than stress about it, I just workout and move my body more. I love walking, so I walk daily. It doesn't make me muscular, but it certainly makes me happy. When it gets colder, I may switch to running and going to the gym. The act alone makes me feel better about myself even if I don't lose one pound. Our bodies change throughout our lives with age, children, and illness, but we still can find ways to adjust to those changes and honor our body.

As cliché as it sounds, we really do have to love ourselves and all our imperfections. What I have noticed is that it makes it hard for others to celebrate us when we don't love ourselves. Sometimes, we meet compliments with self-deprecating statements instead of receiving them graciously.

Unfortunately, I know this is a challenge, especially as women, because we constantly receive messages about how we should look, how we should dress, and how much we should weigh, not to mention all the body trends, modifications, and augmentations that are popular these days. It's hard to love yourself in a world where there are so many mixed messages—be thick, be skinny, or be slim-thick. I think if we leave it up to the world, we will never measure up because there's always something we could do better. We must find a realistic appearance for us that makes us feel good and doesn't put our health at risk. By making space and time for physical activities that nurture how we feel about ourselves, we can begin shifting the inner dialogue that supports us rather than breaks us down.

Take a moment to reflect on how you view your body.

Reflections

1. How can you show your body more love? What do you love most about your appearance?
2. What negative story do you tell yourself about your body? What can you start saying to yourself instead?
3. How can you implement exercise in ways that you enjoy? How many times a week can you exercise?
4. What have you tried, and why hasn't it worked?
5. How does committing to moving your body make you feel?
6. If this is an area in which you excel, take some time to acknowledge your hard work and give yourself a moment of celebration.

CHAPTER 10:

HEALTH CHECK

"Health isn't a goal. It's a way of living."
—Unknown.

How are we fueling our bodies each day? Are you getting enough sleep? Are you getting enough nutrients? Are you drinking water? Are you paying attention to signs that your body is giving you?

This chapter was a tough one for me because it was an area in which I questioned myself. Who am I to talk about health when I had cancer, right? That thought was in a moment, and I had to take time to process. Pre-cancer, I lived a relatively healthy lifestyle. I ate a lot of whole foods with a balanced pescatarian diet. I tried to eat very clean, and I bought fresh farm foods. I didn't eat candy or chips, but I indulged in fresh pastries from time to time at a cafe with friends. I exercised regularly, did yoga, took long walks, and hiked. I never got into smoking, and I only drank alcohol socially.

Then, I received my diagnosis on October 19, 2018, and it made me wonder what the point of my healthy lifestyle was. Why did I work so hard to stay healthy and do all the things that I was supposed to do? I had to sit with that for a while to process it. What I came to realize was that my healthy lifestyle was giving me options. By the time the doctors actually believed me, I was already in stage four of my illness. The cancer had been in my spine, sternum, and abdomen. My oncologist informed me that because of my stage there was usually only one course of action which was an intense chemo regimen that is stronger and more frequent and would for sure leave me infertile with a host of side effects including an increased risk of cancer (what an option). However, because of my health and age, I had another option. I could start with a less aggressive course of treatment and graduate to the aggressive regimen if needed. I took it as a sign, and I was grateful to have a choice where there usually isn't any. I chose to go with the less aggressive option, and I thankfully was able to stay on that course.

> *Visit peaceandsuccess.com to access this free resource:*
> *Health Values Check In*

At that moment, I realized that the healthy lifestyle I was leading was not for nothing because it put me in the best position to fight and recover with "less" damage to my body. Prioritizing ourselves and our health doesn't mean that bad things won't happen. It means you have the best chance of navigating through them. What's interesting is that through my cancer journey, I had multiple people (people who hadn't had cancer before) telling me what I should and shouldn't do or eat. I had to learn how not to take it personally and remember that they do not know what else to do or say. Maybe their counsel was shared out of love. Maybe they really believed that celery juice was going to cure me instantly. Maybe they really believed that if I just ate only this one fruit all day every day, I would be fine. However, given the severity of where I was and given the places where my cancer had spread, I didn't want to take that chance.

It was conflicting for me because I believe in naturopathic medicine. I never thought of having to consider chemotherapy and putting all of those drugs in my body that killed everything good and bad and incurring all of the short and long-term side effects. I would have loved a natural course of treatment; however, given where I was, I didn't have time for that. Subsequently, I had to make a choice that supported me but also aligned with what my values were. What I chose to do was do a combination approach also known as an integrative approach. I had a medical oncologist, but I also had a naturopathic oncologist to support my journey. I found this very empowering, and it didn't make me feel like I had to compromise all my values. I found that during the treatment and after it, medical oncology doesn't really prepare you for what happens next—that is the point where you wonder, *what do I do now? How do I prevent this? What's going to happen to my body in the future?* Naturopathic medicine, however, really is preventative, and I love it. I hope that one day it becomes more integrated into modern medicine.

I also want to say that being vegetarian or vegan does not mean that you're healthy. Eating only protein does not mean that you are healthy. In my opinion, you need balance and adequate nutrients. You need a healthy lifestyle approach that works for you, rather than multiple stressful diets. You don't want something that feels restrictive or something that is a fleeting fad. There always will be some new ideas or trends, and that becomes exhausting and confusing. I will never tell you what you should and shouldn't consume because I am not a dietitian. Food is such a major part of our lives; it's how we break bread, nourish our bodies, and get energy. Find what works for you and your body. Stick to your system and maintain your peace of mind. Find ways to create ease in your dietary lifestyle—perhaps meal prepping or ordering meal kits. Do what serves you and your health.

If this is something with which you struggle, please seek support, or even perform a quick search online that can give you tips. Understand that the food that we eat is what fuels our body to do what it needs to do. In my case, although I was already eating healthy, during treatment, I made some modifications. I removed some of my coffees and alcohol, drank more fresh pressed juices, and increased my fruit and vegetable consumption. In my mind, I had to prepare the troops for battle, so I gave them everything they needed to have the best outcome. You can also think of it as giving your car gas or even the right gas. If you give your car the wrong fuel or a substitute, things can go awry fairly quickly. If we continue to give ourselves poor fuel, how will we run effectively?

Take a moment to reflect on your own health.

Reflections

1. Evaluate what you consume daily or weekly.
2. How often do you incorporate healthy alternatives into your meal?
3. What is your favorite meal? How frequently do you eat it?
4. Pay attention to your body after you've eaten; how do you feel? Our body gives us signs when it doesn't like something, but we don't notice them because we are in a constant state of discomfort.

5. Is there something you know you are overindulging in? What is it?
6. What is your favorite healthy food? Can you find more ways to incorporate it?
7. If this is an area in which you excel, find ways to be at peace with it and celebrate yourself for all your hard work.

CHAPTER 11:

ENVIRONMENTAL SHIFT

"Incredible change happens in your life when you decide to take control of what you do have power over instead of craving control over what you don't." —Steve Maraboli

Where do you go to unwind? What are you consuming on your phone or television? What are the spaces you are entering? What are the conversations you are entertaining? How does music affect your mood?

The year was 2019. It felt like my world was closing in. I had this diagnosis. My mother was paralyzed, and I was navigating this new relationship with her. I planned to move to another country to get my PhD, which now seemed like it would never happen. I then planned to move my mom into a more accessible home, which also was unable to happen. There were instances when I felt stuck, as everything seemed to be very much out of my control. Then, to keep it interesting, we entered a global pandemic. Needless to say, that added an element of challenge in itself. I once had support during my chemotherapy sessions. Now, I had to go to them alone, dodging this deadly virus.

When I came home after treatment, I wasn't feeling like my normal self, maybe because it felt like the house was plagued with illness, but something was not working.

I did what I knew to do, which was to reflect on my options. What do I need right now? What is bothering me the most? I realized I needed a place to unwind–a place for respite; I felt like I didn't have that. Right before we entered the full pandemic, I was able to repurpose one of the bedrooms in my house (on a budget, of course) by throwing out old furniture and getting some paint. I transformed the room and made it into a yoga space. It was somewhat empty, but it was complete with nice, stark white walls with a mirror, a desk in the corner, and my yoga mat in the middle. That was all I had in here. Slowly, I found second-hand pieces like a plant stand and a couch to complement the space, but I was happy, I made it my own, and it's actually where I'm writing this book now.

It is easy to get wrapped up in all that you cannot do, but how much more empowering is it to explore what you can do? During my recovery, I did the same with my bedroom. I did a complete refresh, changed the paint, added some wallpaper, and painted the furniture, and it made a dramatic difference in my sleep and comfort.

In addition to modifying my spaces, I began modifying the things that I was consuming. I started changing the information and the messaging that I was receiving through music, television, and social media. I found a whole new genre of music that was spiritual and grounded in affirmations and manifestations that fostered liberation, love, and peace (I am happy to share my playlists).

Chapter 11: Environmental Shift

> *Visit peaceandsuccess.com to access this free resource:*
> *Supporting Your Internal Environment*

During treatment, I started a yoga certification which opened me up more spiritually than I had ever been previously. When I had been doing yoga in the past, the emphasis was on the asanas, which are physical movements. What I really loved was what was off the mat practice–what happened to the mind and how I interacted with myself and the world. Starting my yoga teacher training allowed me to dive deeply into principles that aligned with me, and I am sure that those principles have influenced this book greatly.

In addition to my yoga certification, I completed two coaching certifications. This was an area in which I wanted to learn more, and with my psychology background, I was so interested in how they differed. The information was comprehensive, and it shifted my focus from the things I could not control to a place where I was educating myself and learning a new skill. I loved it, and I still do. Coaching aligns with who I am, and it allows me to empower others and support them in a systematic way to achieve their dreams. I have my own practice now where, like in this book, I help women prioritize themselves to identify obstacles that are keeping them from achieving their goals. I use peace as a success principle where we uncover areas of your life that are conflicting with your peace of mind and are limiting your mental capacity to focus on the life you want. Receiving my certification in coaching was one of the best decisions I made for myself during that challenging time because I see it as a gift–one that I literally can share with others for the rest of my life.

> *Visit peaceandsuccess.com to learn more about my coaching practice and how I can help you or email me at connect@kenishahanson.com*

As I mentioned, I loved journaling, but during treatment, I started becoming more intentional about the focus of my journal entries. Instead of just recapping my challenges or thoughts of the day, I would open with gratitude and the positive things that happened in my day. I would make it feel lighter, not to ignore or suppress the feelings that might come up but to find more space to share the things that were good, funny, and enjoyable. There was so much I could complain about, and it felt like I was being chased by a dark cloud, but I was determined to stay in the light, so I kept moving, immersing myself in activities, practices, and education that enriched my soul. I had to keep the balance, modifying my external world to support my internal work. If I was doing all these reflective practices only to consume nothing but negative media, I constantly would be conflicted, and I never truly would be at peace. To me that is like pouring water into a bucket with holes in it.

I think sometimes we don't realize what we're letting in from our environment and how that impacts us. While sometimes it feels like we don't have control of our environment when we take a minute to reflect, there's usually something that we can do that can give us peace. It doesn't have to be a whole remodel, or we do not have to move to another country or only listen to ocean waves, but it's important that we evaluate what's entering our minds, when it is entering our minds, and what we feel when we enter spaces. Are we spending time in natural environments that support us both mentally and physically?

Take a moment to reflect on your own environment.

Reflections

1. Evaluate your external environment and places you frequent.
2. Do you feel at home when you're at home? What can you add to improve your mood? Can you add a plant or nightstand? You would be surprised how little convenience can improve your state of mind.
3. Have you evaluated your social media? Is it curated with only things that interest you? Do you engage with content that supports your peace of mind?
4. Where and when do you feel most at peace? I ask that you don't choose to rely on a vacation because it is important that we don't get caught in destination happiness—I will be happy when I get this or when I get that. Focus on what's in front of us. We can desire things, but we shouldn't delay our happiness until we get them.
5. If this is an area where you excel, take a minute to sit in your space and express gratitude for where you are and what you have been able to do for yourself.

PART FIVE
SUCCESS

CHAPTER 12:

MAINTAIN YOUR PEACE

"Love and peace of mind do protect us; they allow us to overcome the problems that life hands us. They teach us to survive, to live now, to have the courage to confirm each day."
—Bernie Siegel.

Before delving into the topic of success, let's take a moment to talk about maintaining your inner peace. Life has an interesting way of making us forget the very things that bring us joy and contentment when we're feeling good. We often neglect the practices and habits that contribute to our happiness because, well, we're already in a good place. But here's the thing – we're in that good place precisely because of those practices.

It's essential to stay connected to what makes you laugh, what brings a smile to your face, and what makes you feel good about yourself. These are the elements that support your overall well-being and peace of mind. Reading a self-help book and feeling inspired for a moment or even a day isn't enough. Real change demands commitment and effort. We humans are creatures of habit, and we tend to stick to our routines, even when they no longer serve us because it's what we have been doing. If we're not mindful of our needs, we can unintentionally continue down a path that doesn't align with our desires, all the while wondering why we're not where we want to be.

I vividly remember the time during chemotherapy when I sought the help of a psychologist, as recommended by my medical oncologist. To be honest, I didn't find it helpful at all. I struggled to connect with the therapist, feeling there was a cultural barrier, and that she didn't truly understand me. I possess the ability to express myself and work through challenges, but that doesn't imply I don't encounter difficulties. Interestingly, this ability has sometimes presented a challenge in itself. It can give the impression that I'm effortlessly handling everything, which can, in turn, result in less concern or care being directed towards me and this situation was no different.

When I decided to seek therapy, my primary goal was to have a neutral space where I could explore my thoughts and emotions openly, and ultimately feel supported. However, after sharing my story, the therapist abruptly informed me that I wasn't depressed, even though I hadn't mentioned depression at all. I was merely dealing with a lot on my plate and wanted an impartial outlet to help me navigate. To my surprise, she suggested that I couldn't continue caring for my mom and implied I should place her in a care facility.

As my mom's only child, I didn't have the option to stop caring for her. Who else would take care of her if not me? Is it tough sometimes? Absolutely. Do I miss the dynamic we had in our relationship before? Of course. However, should I now move her to a residence with people 15 to 20 years older than she is, while I watch her deteriorate? What would be the cost, not just financially, but mentally, emotionally, and in terms of her well-being? It felt like an insensitive solution that didn't consider the overall impact on both our health and well-being. The therapist offered no tools or guidance; instead, she told me that I couldn't continue caring for my mom, asserting that I wasn't depressed and that I was well-adjusted. Needless to say, I didn't return for another session. Please don't misunderstand – I firmly believe in the value of therapy. Remember, I had aspired to become a therapist myself. I had hoped that therapy would be beneficial, but unfortunately, my experience fell far short of that.

Fortunately, during my cancer journey, I attended a weekend retreat with Pink Pearl, an organization for adolescents and young adults with cancer, often referred to as AYA. It was there that I encountered a therapist who seemed much better equipped to understand my concerns. This therapist was down-to-earth, informed, and knowledgeable. At the time, I didn't feel an immediate need for therapy, or perhaps I still had some reservations from the previous therapist's session. Nonetheless, I took note of the therapist's contact information, just in case I felt differently in the future.

As I neared the end of my treatment, things became increasingly challenging. The thing about chemotherapy is that its effects compound, so the more sessions you undergo, the worse you feel. This is especially true in my experience, and it takes a cumulative toll on your body. My appointments grew more painful, and the drugs started affecting my heart. I found myself in and out of the hospital while dealing with the challenges of the COVID-19 pandemic, which posed an elevated risk to both my life and my mother's. Moreover, I was denied the comfort of having a support person with me during these trying times. Needless to say, this was an exceptionally tough period, not only on a personal level but also as I observed all that was happening in the world. I did my best to keep it together, ensuring my mom's safety while practicing mindfulness and staying focused on things outside of the moment, such as my certifications.

The day finally arrived when I received the news of my remission. However, it wasn't at all as joyous as I had expected. I didn't skip down the hallway with happiness or even dance! Instead, I felt an unusual indifference. On one hand, I was relieved that I had survived – I did it, yay me! On the other hand, I couldn't help but wonder, w*hat now*?

As time passed, I began to notice that something wasn't quite right. I was going through the motions of my daily routines, like my walks and journaling, but an underlying sense of uncertainty about my identity lingered. I didn't know how to shake it off. I felt stuck. There were days, more like a few, when I considered deleting all my pre-cancer photos because I no longer recognized the person in them. The more I dwelled on what used to be, the more it seemed to hold me back, stealing my joy. It became evident that I couldn't overcome this challenge on my own.

I reached out to the therapist I had met at the AYA cancer program late one night, around 11:00 p.m. to be exact. Remarkably, I received a prompt response by morning, offering their support as my therapist. We embarked on a journey to explore the grief of my past self – a concept that was entirely foreign to me. It turns out, this experience is quite common. Essentially, you mourn the person you were before and grapple with uncertainty about the person you've become.

Chapter 12: Maintain Your Peace

In my case I wanted to be that person again. My body had changed, and I had lost my physical strength. My mind was different, and I had way more emotional expression than I ever had. I no longer recognized the person I once was. With the help of my therapist, I embarked on a journey to move through this challenging period and to learn to love and embrace the new me. I didn't need to discard my past self; instead, I needed to make space for the person I had become. I needed time to get to know the aspects of myself that I thought I had already understood.

This experience taught me the importance of having a plan when life's challenges feel overwhelming. Whether it's a therapist, a supportive friend, or a place of worship, having a plan in place ensures that you know where to turn when you need support. The journey toward a peaceful life is a beautiful one, but it necessitates introspection and self-discovery. You must define and redefine your needs and learn to love yourself unconditionally.

Maintaining certain activities keeps us grounded and connected to ourselves. It gives us the structure we need to overcome obstacles as they arise, but it also gives us the clarity to stay committed to our goals and thrive. Challenges are an inherent part of life, and they come in various forms. It might not be cancer or grief for everyone, but we all have our unique stories that impact us. The question is, how are we moving through that story and beyond to give ourselves the life we want?

I often reflect on how different my story might have been if I hadn't chosen to continue showing up or develop a system for nurturing peace of mind while caring for my paralyzed mother during my cancer journey. Your system, the one I hope you will take the time to curate from principles in this book, will enable you to prioritize yourself and your needs, empowering you to achieve and live your success story—one firmly grounded in peace. Success, whatever it means to you, is well within your reach. However, it demands that you make specific choices aligned with your well-being and your own definition of success.

As Albert Einstein wisely said, 'Peace cannot be kept by force. It can only be achieved by understanding,' and to me, that means a deep understanding of oneself.

Take a moment to reflect on your own maintenance journey.

Reflections:

1. What are some activities or practices that make you feel genuinely good about yourself, and how frequently do you engage in them?
2. How do you typically respond to life's challenges, and are you open to making changes to overcome them more effectively?
3. Have you ever had a negative experience with therapy, and if so, what insights did you gain from it?
4. How do you cope with significant life changes, especially those that challenge your sense of identity or create uncertainty about the future?
5. What strategies do you have in place for seeking support when you feel overwhelmed, and how successful have they been in the past?

Chapter 12: Maintain Your Peace

6. How do you create space for the evolving version of yourself as you grow and change over time, and what are some of the challenges you face in this process?

7. In what ways can love and inner peace serve as protective factors in dealing with life's challenges, and how can you actively incorporate these qualities into your life?

CHAPTER 13:

SUCCESS STORY

> "Success should not be a race to impress others but a path
> to express your authentic self."
> —Unknown

What is your definition of Success? Who has influenced this definition? Does your definition reflect your goals and your strengths?

As you embark on part five of this book, it's time to delve into the concept of success. We've discussed various aspects of finding peace, but how does success tie into all of this? What does success truly mean? In my experience, success is a term often burdened by societal expectations, loaded with "should," and accompanied by specific career choices, wealth, and status goals. Society often dictates that you should become a doctor, lawyer, and achieve a certain financial status by a certain age. However, upon closer examination or just observing the life of celebrities, we find that these external markers, such as wealth and status, do not guarantee inner contentment. In fact, they can often exacerbate inner conflicts rather than resolve them. True success

Chapter 13: Success Story

transcends societal definitions and material achievements. It's about discovering genuine contentment and fulfillment in our lives.

So, what do we do? As we've explored in the first four parts of this book, it all begins with introspection. Take the time to assess how your definition of success has evolved over time and whether it aligns with your goals and strengths. What might have constituted success when you were a child or in high school may hold a different meaning for you now.

When I was growing up, I encountered the same messages many of us do. The path to success seemed straightforward: get an education, secure a good job, and then add marriage and children to the mix, and you've achieved it all. This path often offers limited and predetermined choices. Anything outside the preconceived notions of a "good" career is often overlooked or dismissed. These societal expectations shape our worldview and influence our aspirations. If you're reading this and have managed to forge your own unique path, defying conventional wisdom, I am so happy for you and I genuinely applaud your courage. I understand that it might not have been an easy journey, depending on your upbringing, and it's a significant reason why many of us just end up conforming. After all, adults are supposed to know better, right?

Wrong. As I matured, I began to realize that our parents and elders, while sharing their wisdom, also carried their own limitations. They often asked fewer questions and accepted the status quo more readily than we do now. There seemed to be an expectation to "do as you're told, not as I do," and disagreement hardly seemed like an option. Of course, this doesn't apply to everyone and doesn't account for social movements that challenged norms. However, from my perspective as a first-generation Canadian with Jamaican heritage, this was very much my reality. Our parents' experiences shaped their perspectives, and while they possess wisdom, they may not fully comprehend what is best for us in the context of this generation or the vast possibilities that exist beyond their understanding.

I've mentioned before in my personal journey that I grew up with a comfortable life, largely unaware of our financial struggles. We weren't wealthy, as we received government assistance and lived in cooperative housing, but I had what I needed. What I did know was that my mom worked tirelessly, often holding down two jobs, and there was an expectation for me to excel in school. Like many of us, this expectation was stated explicitly and frequently. I saw my dad on weekends, sometimes he would show up, other times he promised to and didn't. It was during these moments that I began crafting a narrative in my head that maybe the better I performed academically, the prouder he would be of me, which would translate into him being more present in my life.

Report card after report card, praise after praise, it all began to define my identity - I had to be smart. By the time I reached high school, my grades had become the barometer of my self-worth, and in my mind, my career choices narrowed down to becoming either a lawyer or a psychologist because I enjoyed those fields out of the ones deemed acceptable and it would make my mom happy. Graduating with scholarships, I set my sights on obtaining a PhD. It wasn't just a desire; it was a need - a need to validate my worthiness. My narrative became centered around being intelligent, and anything that challenged that notion threatened my very identity.

Chapter 13: Success Story

Naturally, I went on to complete my Master of Science and had the opportunity to do it in the UK, so the next step was the big one. I was almost there. However, as you know, life took an unexpected turn when my mother was diagnosed with a severe autoimmune disorder while I simultaneously received an offer to pursue my PhD overseas. I had invested so much effort in that application, meticulously selecting the perfect advisor with additional support from advisors who also believed in my research. I did explore other options, considering different schools and potential advisors, but none of them felt like the perfect fit. When you're embarking on a three to four-year journey with them, alignment is crucial. As I mentioned, I decided to defer for a year, thinking everything would be fine by then. But I was wrong.

The following year, I was eager to embark on the journey to my doctorate, but my mother's health had not improved, and I was further halted by my own diagnosis of Stage IV Hodgkin's Lymphoma. I still vividly remember having to send that email, informing them that I would be unable to attend. I couldn't even fathom the words I was typing. I thought to myself, "My advisor must think I'm making up this dramatic story." It felt like a cruel joke, as if reality couldn't possibly be this challenging. I had put in so much hard work, established connections, and poured my heart into my aspirations, only to watch it all crumble before my eyes.

At that moment, I was devastated. It felt like a loss of self, for I had tied my entire identity to this pursuit of success. Without my PhD, I questioned the purpose of all my efforts. Was I now a failure? Useless? It took time for me to peel away the layers of attachment and realize that my success story had been entwined with external factors aimed at filling an internal void. I had to be brutally honest with myself, acknowledging my insecurities and being open to the possibility of crafting a new narrative. Unpacking all of this was extraordinarily difficult, exceptionally so. But I will take you on this journey.

My PhD had become the pinnacle of success for me because it would grant me the title of "doctor," it would grant me access to academia, and, ultimately, it was an outward indicator of my intelligence. It all seemed perfectly logical, right? On the surface, it did. However, now that I had cancer and was a full-time caregiver, pursuing my PhD was no longer a feasible option, and that's where my struggle began. I simply could not let it go.

Let's dig deeper. I had professed that my PhD was an indicator of my intelligence because, honestly, I had never truly considered myself exceptionally smart. I was often surprised when I received good grades. The areas where I struggled, like math, consistently made me doubt my overall abilities, no matter how many A's I earned. I harbored a deep need to be perfect or at least perceived as such. I always believed I could do better and learn more quickly than I was.

Let's delve even further. I also tethered my self-worth to this pursuit of higher education. I believed that obtaining my PhD would make me undeniable - that I would be worth loving, worth showing up for, especially in the eyes of my father, and later, worth respecting as a Black woman in the world. It was incredibly layered, intricately woven into the fabric of my existence, and, as I write this now, I doubt I would have fully comprehended it unless it had all unraveled before my eyes or not until much later in life.

Chapter 13: Success Story

So, how did I rediscover my path? Truthfully, I had to take a step back, carefully examine all the facts, and engage in numerous conversations with myself - and my therapist. I had to remind myself that everything I had accomplished up to that point was not invalidated simply because I didn't have my PhD. There was no possible way that I was now a failure or considered useless just because I couldn't achieve this one thing. My story had been erroneously tied to external factors attempting to fill an internal void. Being open and honest about my insecurities, even if just to myself, was the first step toward freeing myself from this story and creating space for a new one. And did I mention therapy? It was a crucial part of my journey.

Sometimes, I wonder what would have happened if I had achieved my dream of studying overseas and earned those letters beside my name. Would I have truly found happiness or validation from those whose approval I sought? Perhaps not. Insecurities might have persisted, and I might have continued moving the goalposts, seeking even grander achievements to prove my worth. Through introspection and conversations with others who have faced similar experiences, I've come to understand the power of self-awareness and reflection.

Today, my definition of success has evolved. While I still aspire to pursue higher education in this lifetime, I've disentangled it from my sense of self-worth and from being the sole measure of success. Today, success is a blend of inner growth, living a life that aligns with my desires, needs, and wants, and maintaining the awareness to pivot when necessary. It entails granting myself grace and honoring who I am and where I am in my journey. It's truly about my relationship with myself. As I reflect on it now, in the face of a life-threatening illness, I was once saddened by my inability to pursue my doctorate. It may sound trivial, I'm sure. But that's the power these stories have - they weave themselves deep into our core. Only we can unravel them through honest reflection, letting go of what no longer serves us, and creating space for personal growth.

Understanding the origins of these stories and the weight they carry in our lives is crucial. They have the power to shape our beliefs, influence our choices, and hinder our true potential. By questioning our definition of success, we liberate ourselves from the constraints of societal norms and expectations. We open ourselves up to a new paradigm of success, one that aligns with our values, brings us peace of mind, and fosters genuine fulfillment.

Take a moment now to reflect on your own journey.

Reflection

1. When was the last time you evaluated and questioned your definition of success? Whose story are you living?
2. How does your current definition of success align with your values and bring you peace of mind?
3. Have you ever felt unhappy or unfulfilled despite achieving what society deems as success? Reflect on that experience.
4. What aspects of your current definition of success do you want to let go of? What new aspects do you want to embrace?
5. In the quest for success, remember that your journey is uniquely yours, and it's okay to redefine success on your terms.

CHAPTER 14:

REDEFINING SUCCESS

"Redefining success means having the courage to let go of what no longer serves you and embracing what brings you true happiness."
— Unknown

How would you define success if it were not influenced by societal expectations and external factors?

This chapter could easily be titled "Redefining Success with Grace, Self-Love, and Compassion," but that would have been far too long. As you embark on this journey, it's essential to discuss how to put these principles into practice. After all, there's no point in reading this book if you don't have a plan to implement the teachings, build your toolkit, and apply these concepts to your life. Let's start with a fundamental truth: this process may not always be easy, and you might even question yourself as this new definition of success begins to take shape.

As you deepen your relationship with yourself and establish your boundaries, there may be moments when you encounter resistance from others or feel like you don't fit the societal mold. But remember, you are not meant to conform; you are here to create your path and dream beyond the limitations that others may attempt to impose upon you.

To put this all into perspective, let me share a couple of stories and my personal reflections on them. I previously mentioned that when I went into remission, I didn't really celebrate. It was a strange time for me because I was striving so hard to return to what I considered "normal." However, I failed to realize that this was my new normal. Things were changing, and I was changing, but I was still operating with a pre-cancer mindset and pre-cancer goals. At first, I thought I still wanted the titles and accolades. I had worked so diligently to reach that point, right? Yet, when the dust settled, I felt that something no longer aligned. It took time for me to understand that I had become a different person with a different operating system.

When it came to my career, I used to be completely focused on the traditional path, striving for numerous titles and accolades. However, my perspective had shifted dramatically. While I always knew I didn't want to work until the age of 65, I had also aspired to accumulate all the titles and accomplishments that could fit on a resume. But then, I'd often overhear conversations where people openly expressed their dissatisfaction with their jobs but continued on solely for the sake of their pension. To me, it felt like settling, a never-ending cycle of unhappiness and mediocrity. Let me clarify, I'm not here to judge anyone's choices or question their decisions. This was simply about what I envisioned for the trajectory of my own life.

I realized I no longer dreamed of working in the traditional sense; instead, I yearned for experiences and impact. This shift marked the

Chapter 14: Redefining Success

beginning of my coaching journey. I recognized that I possessed a unique gift and a story that could help other women embrace self-care, nurture their souls, and achieve their personal and professional goals. This was foundational, life-changing work.

However, I encountered a significant difference in support when I transitioned from the traditional 9-5 job to entrepreneurship. While pursuing my education, my family celebrated my academic achievements. Even my dentist was aware of my pursuit of a master's degree; it was the talk of the town. However, when I pivoted toward my business, venturing into entrepreneurship, and coaching instead of counseling, becoming an author rather than a distinguished researcher, and reevaluating my desire to have children, everything changed. The energy shifted; people around me didn't understand. I heard comments like, "You have a good job and an education, what else do you need?" No one explicitly said I shouldn't pursue this new direction, but there wasn't much enthusiasm either. I noticed subtle redirections or questions like, "What about your pension?" and expressions of disbelief, such as "Don't worry; you'll change your mind about having kids."

Even my mother, who is typically my biggest cheerleader, grew quiet. I couldn't hear her cheering anymore. For so long, my path had been clear: I was going to be a doctor with all the accolades and titles. Now, I had decided I wanted to be an author and run my coaching business. I wanted to work for myself, empower women to prioritize their peace, and redefine success on their terms. It was an entirely new direction, and it didn't make sense to her. She couldn't wrap her head around it. I'll be honest; I was initially hurt by her lack of enthusiasm. But when I reflected on it, I had to ask myself how she could cheer for something she had never seen before. She had held dreams for me for so long, and I was letting them go. She didn't understand entrepreneurship; I barely did myself. How could she relate to it when it was entirely outside her realm of experience? Sometimes we expect the people in our lives to believe in something beyond their capabilities or understanding. We ask them to believe in a seed that hasn't yet been planted. Sometimes they need to see it and experience it before they can offer their support. Is it unfortunate? Yes. Is it disappointing? Absolutely. But your success story has to be your own. Your dreams and passions must be fulfilled by you. Sometimes the lack of support or pushback may discourage us and lead us to abandon our dreams prematurely. You might be the one who has to pave the way for others to see that it can be done.

I share this because sometimes your story won't align with what someone has envisioned for you. They might only see you one way, which can hinder their ability to see beyond the life they've outlined for you. That's why it's crucial to connect with who you are, reflect on what you need, and ensure that no one else defines your path for you. This also means being clear about your boundaries and knowing what you believe in, so you can navigate and withstand anything and anyone who challenges your ideas or depletes your energy. I can say now that, as my mother saw my vision come to life, she has become my biggest supporter. She attends all my events, tells her friends about my business, and shares my story with anyone who will listen. She can see it now and understands how and why it suits me. But she wasn't prepared for what I had to say next.

If no longer pursuing a conventional job wasn't enough, I also decided that I might not want to have children. This decision had a more profound impact on everyone around me than I anticipated. It was as though I was shattering their dream—especially when it came to my family. However, for me, it was a complex and deeply emotional matter.

So why did I suddenly decide that I might not want children? To be honest, it stemmed from fear, primarily the fear of cancer recurrence. I wondered, what if I had children, and then the cancer returned? The thought of my hypothetical children seeing me in that condition or potentially losing me filled me with profound sadness. I also questioned whether it was even possible for me to have children given my medical history. The doctors assured me that, given my treatment, I should be fine, but they couldn't offer a guarantee. Before undergoing a series of chemotherapy sessions, I faced the choice of freezing my eggs or potentially losing them forever. I chose to freeze my eggs. There wasn't much time for discussion with my partner; it had to be done then or not at all. The process was far from what I expected; it was neither a vacation nor a painless procedure.

For those unfamiliar with the process, let me share a brief overview of my experience. To begin, you have to prepare your eggs for retrieval, which involves about two weeks of self-administered abdominal injections. You visit the doctor every few days for ultrasounds to ensure everything is proceeding as planned. When they determine there are enough eggs or that they are mature enough (although don't quote me on that), they initiate the extraction process. I vividly remember the day of the procedure. The doctor assured me it would be a short, painless, outpatient procedure where I would remain awake but sedated and should not feel anything. However, during the procedure, there were complications with the alignment of my ovaries, and the sedation didn't fully work for me. I could feel everything that was happening, and I recall nurses urgently trying to adjust my ovaries. I lay there, holding my best friend's hand, stunned that I could feel everything. She recognized something was wrong right away and informed them that I was in pain. They halted the procedure and administered more sedatives. Once they confirmed I could no longer feel anything, they completed the extraction and collected a number of eggs which are now frozen.

I'm extremely grateful that I had the opportunity to freeze my eggs before undergoing chemotherapy, and I'm thankful that egg freezing is an option. However, I've come to understand that it's not as straightforward as people often make it sound. There's a prevailing notion that you can "just" undergo reproductive treatments, but there are no guarantees, and it comes with a significant financial cost. Despite the overwhelming simplifications we hear, many women can attest that there is nothing "just" about it. The mental, physical, emotional, and financial toll can be incredibly challenging. Therefore, if I can offer one piece of advice, it's this: be mindful and respectful of women and their reproductive choices and challenges. I didn't even complete the entire process, and it caused me significant distress at various points along the way.

Over time, despite my declarations that I wouldn't have children, part of me still held onto the desire. However, I struggled with guilt and questioned whether I was being selfish by wanting to bring life into this world. I wondered if I would be doing them a disservice given my own and my mother's medical histories. It seemed like a lot of family history to impose on hypothetical children. My desire to have a family of my own also stemmed from my own fragmented family experience. I wanted my children to grow up in a loving and supportive family unit. So, was it about family or filling a void? Perhaps a bit of both, but predominantly the latter. Underlying it all was a yearning for what I felt I lacked. This is where self-reflection and awareness became paramount because I had to sit with these thoughts and conflicting ideas to free myself from the mental turmoil. I had to give myself permission to not have all the answers, to change my mind, to grow, and to desire different things at various stages of my life. I had gone through an experience that completely turned my world upside down. I do know that many people have children before and after a cancer diagnosis, and everything turns out fine. However, this was about my experience. I needed to grant myself grace to potentially diverge from societal norms and what I thought my life would be. Bringing life into the world cannot and should not solely define who I am. I am not less of a person, no matter what I choose. While parenthood can be a beautiful gift, it can also be challenging, and it is not obligatory.

Ultimately, for the sake of my peace, I felt it was necessary to release my attachment to the idea of giving birth to children. It had placed a tremendous amount of pressure on me, and I couldn't control the outcome. While I hoped for the possibility of having children naturally, I needed to reach a place where I was content without that possibility.

So, how do you release the weight of expectations and free yourself from societal guilt and pressure? By now, you likely know the answer: it begins with self-awareness, reflection, and evaluation. However, it's not enough to reflect; you must apply everything we've discussed in the first four parts of this book.

- Take the time to assess what you genuinely want, why you want it, and how it aligns with your values and aspirations.
- Examine the facets of your life and determine how they either support or drain you.
- Identify and commit to the actions necessary to facilitate change or release what no longer serves you.
- Recognize the aspects of your current definition of success that no longer align with your life's trajectory and remain open to embracing new perspectives and dreams.
- Take the time to develop a beautiful relationship with yourself and consistently nurture that relationship.

For example, I once believed I desperately needed a PhD to support my career aspirations, but it had also become intertwined with my insecurities, self-worth, and the need for validation from others. When I disentangled these elements, I realized it's not inherently wrong to aspire to achieve a PhD; however, it's problematic to believe that my self-worth and the love and respect I receive from my father are contingent upon obtaining those letters before my name. My father's capacity to express love for me will remain the same, as it reflects his experiences and the work he chooses to do or not to do. I cannot hinge my self-worth or attempt to use external achievements to motivate internal change in another person. I will take responsibility for my feelings and growth, freeing myself from the vortex of another's behavior and experiences. I will honor myself by knowing who I am and living in alignment with my desires, needs, and aspirations as they are and may become. I will embrace the power of inner peace to anchor myself in a fulfilled life, both personally and professionally.

Chapter 14: Redefining Success

I know I've just covered a lot there, but I want you to grasp the significance of unpacking your thoughts, progressing toward inner peace, and reshaping your definition of success from a place of wholeness and self-love.

For me, making this shift involved reevaluating a long-held dream and goal. I realized how this aspiration had influenced my thoughts, shaped my self-perception, and imposed limits on my life. Today, I oversee a peace centered community, guiding women from around the world to prioritize self-care, love themselves, and break free from lifestyles that no longer serve them. My dedication lies in helping them uncover their values and discover the incredible potential within themselves. However, to do so effectively, I must continue to grow and commit to myself. This transformation doesn't happen after a single journal entry or a session of deep breathing. We are continually evolving and experiencing life, which means we must consistently put in the work. It's about cultivating and sustaining a connection with yourself, discovering new ways to honor and love who you are. Think of it as nurturing a friendship. You don't establish a friendship and then communicate with that person only once for the rest of your lives. You invest time to hang out, converse, laugh, cry, celebrate, and share everything in between.

To fully embrace your redefined success, I encourage you to practice living the life you dream of. Embody your vision and summon the courage to decline things that don't serve you or align with this dream. Visualize where you are, what you are doing, how it feels, what you are wearing, what you are eating, who is around you, and the impact you are making. Dedicate yourself to nurturing your mind, soul, and body each day, immersing yourself in the intricacies of your dream life. Dive deep into your story so that you can see it clearly and begin molding it into your reality.

As we approach the end of this book, my hope is that you've found more than just a story about cancer. I hope you've discovered a message of hope and inspiration on your journey toward inner peace and success. I hope you understand that, with your willpower and practice, you can overcome any obstacle that comes your way. By prioritizing your own needs and nurturing your inner peace, you have the power to redefine success on your terms and create a life that aligns with your values and aspirations.

I encourage you to revisit this book time and time again and apply the lessons and insights you've gained to your own life. It may not always be perfect or easy, and doubts may surface along the way, but that's natural. Remember to trust yourself and embrace the journey. This book has equipped you with the tools and insights needed to create a life that aligns with your truest self. The community is here to support you, but it all begins with you. When you connect with your inner self, you unlock your full potential and achieve the greatness you deserve. Always remember that you have the power to find peace on your path to success, and in doing so, you can pave the way for health, wealth, happiness, and fulfillment. You can, and you will, achieve all that you set out to accomplish. Embrace peace as your priority, and watch your dreams become a reality!

To close this book, take a moment to reflect on your own definition of success.

Chapter 14: Redefining Success

Reflection

1. How do external factors, such as familial expectations and societal pressures, influence your perception of success?
2. How can you redefine success to include personal growth, well-being, and inner peace as essential components?
3. What role does self-worth play in your definition of success? How can you redefine success from a place of self-love?
4. What values and principles do you want to guide your redefined version of success?
5. Are you open to changing your mind and exploring new paths as you redefine success? How can you give yourself permission to do so?
6. How can you honor your decisions and navigate the challenges that arise when redefining success?
7. What level of belief do you have in achieving the success you have defined?

   What can you do to strengthen those beliefs daily?
8. What dreams have you set aside or dismissed in the past due to societal pressures? How can you resurrect and pursue them now?
9. How will you take the first step towards aligning your life with your redefined version of success, starting today?
10. What actions can you commit to that will nurture your self-worth and inner peace, ensuring they remain at the core of your journey to success?

11. Take 5 minutes to envision the extraordinary possibilities that await you when you prioritize your peace and define success on your own terms.

    Write down that vision and come back to it daily.

EPILOGUE

Congratulations on reaching the end of this book. You've shown up for yourself, which was the first step, but now you must commit to the actions needed to make a change. You have the tools you need to reflect and evaluate the facets of your life that may be holding you back from achieving the success and fulfillment you want. We underestimate just how much chaos and disconnect from our true selves, distracts us from achieving our goals and experiencing life. When you implement these strategies, you'll be able to acquire the peace of mind you need to curate your experiences and focus on your present. Using peace as a foundational principle allows you to show up as your best self and navigate life's inevitable challenges. It's important that you don't put this book back on the shelf; use it as a reference guide and be sure to download the free resource kit I've made available for you. If you require more personalized assistance, please don't hesitate to contact me. I am here to support you.

> *Visit peaceandsuccess.com for exclusive access to your free resource kit and for more information on how to connect with me.*

Choosing to wait to make a change means you're choosing to stay exactly where you are and allowing the world to deplete you at its leisure. Choosing to wait means you have less time and energy to focus on your dreams and more time in discomfort. Through the reflective practices detailed in this book, you will gain control of your life, define your needs, and step into your worth. I should caution you that making these changes will have a direct impact on you and those who enter and stay in your life. Your energy will change, and the opportunities and individuals you attract will change. Your boundaries may make people uncomfortable, but it's important you honor yourself by honoring your boundaries. It's time to proceed with peace of mind, so you can give to the ones you love and what you love. You are already great. I repeat, you are already great. You can be everything that you want to be, but you have to believe it, define it, and know that you're worth it.

The following is a summary of the concepts in the book to start living your most peaceful and successful life.

Part One: Finances

Chapter 1 - Getting Personal

This chapter highlights how your story about finances influences your habits, behaviors, and your perceived worth. This chapter opens you up to being honest with yourself about the current state of your finances and the direction in which you want to go.

Chapter 2 - Empower Yourself

This chapter is where you identify what you know and need to know to move into an informed position with a financial plan. It reviews the fundamental wealth strategy to prepare you for the present and future.

Epilogue

Chapter 3 - Career Alignment

This chapter helps you evaluate your career and its impact on your identity. It helps you take an inventory of how much energy you give to thinking about where you want to be and define the actions needed to get there.

Part Two: Mental Well-being

Chapter 4 - Allow Yourself in

This chapter is designed to help you take on the challenge of self-reflection. By evaluating your internal dialogue and understanding your perspectives, you can gain insight into how you show up for yourself on a daily basis.

Chapter 5 - Higher Power

This chapter explores the role of faith and spirituality in your life and provides guidance for how you can combat the ebbs and flows of life.

Part Three: Interconnections

Chapter 6 - Know Your Presence

This chapter helps you understand how you relate to others and gives insights into how you contribute to the mutual fulfillment of your relationships.

Chapter 7 - Family and Friends

This chapter helps you clarify your boundaries and reflect on the relationships with your family and friends and the way they may be supporting your journey or taking away from it.

Chapter 8 - Romantic Relationships

Intimate relationships and the pursuit of them can impact how we view ourselves, the heights we reach, and the limitations we experience. This chapter helps you evaluate what you want and how you deserve to be loved.

Part Four: Physical Health

Chapter 9 - Body Image

There is always a story you tell yourself about your body that feels heightened in the digital age. This chapter helps you reflect and create a new story to honor your present and commit to supportive actions.

Chapter 10 -Health Check

Without our health, nothing matters. This chapter helps you evaluate your habits and what is the best supportive course of action to fuel your body.

Chapter 11 - Environmental Shift

This chapter discusses curating your experience with the physical world and controlling what you consume to support your internal work.

Epilogue

Part Five: Success

Chapter 12 - Maintain your Peace

The journey of peace and reflection is not without challenges. This chapter helps you create a plan to support you when life feels out of control.

Chapter 13 - Success Story

This chapter delves into redefining success beyond societal expectations and external markers. The chapter encourages readers to reflect on their own paths and consider a definition of success grounded in personal values and inner fulfillment.

Chapter 14 - Redefining Success

This chapter emphasizes the importance of self-awareness, reflection, and taking deliberate actions to reshape one's definition of success to create a life that aligns with personal desires and aspirations.

Now, it's your moment to embrace peace and alignment, and the first step is self-commitment. You hold the power to define your needs and determine your worth. Clear the path for peace and liberate your mind to explore the possibilities and experience your greatness.

The time has come to Peace Your Way to Success.

PEACE YOUR WAY TO SUCCESS REFLECTIONS

Below, you'll find the reflection questions that appeared throughout this book. Feel free to revisit these prompts whenever needed, allowing them to guide you through various phases of your life. Remember, there are no perfect answers to these questions, and the journey of self-discovery can sometimes be challenging. However, each reflection brings you one step closer to understanding yourself and living a life that aligns with your deepest desires. Embrace the discomfort as a sign of growth and transformation. Your path to peace and success is uniquely yours, and with each step, you're creating a brighter, more fulfilling future. Keep going and trust yourself.

Chapter 1 - Getting Personal

Reflections

1. Evaluate your money story for your starting point. It's okay not to have it right. However, acknowledging and understanding what you want and don't know are the first steps to improving your situation.

2. It's okay to go outside your networks and learn information. Think about where you can go to improve your knowledge. Saving for an emergency fund was only one part of my finances; I had to figure out what was next.
3. In what area of your personal finances are you skilled, or what do you want to learn more about?

Chapter 2 - Empower Yourself

Reflections

1. Identify what you want to know. Educate yourself with some baseline knowledge and seek out experts or take the time to learn for yourself.
2. Learn and commit to immediate action. If my paperwork had gone through a few days earlier. I would have had money to help me through treatment.
3. Share with those who are **ready** to receive information and have conversations or engage in resources about the subject matter. For example, listen to podcasts and thought leaders.

    This does not mean you have to share with the world because not everyone wants to hear that you're getting it together, but you may have a few people with whom you want to ride with you to the top. This is just a suggestion, but it empowered me, solidified my understanding, and made me feel good about sharing the knowledge I learned. We're not here to hoard knowledge, but we also don't need to burden ourselves with people who aren't ready and will discourage us from making the necessary changes in our life.

4. Ask yourself, "What am I most excited to learn?" The world of personal finance is vast. While it seems overwhelming, there could be spaces where you will excel. Figure out what they are and empower yourself to explore the possibilities.

Chapter 3 - Career Alignment

Reflections

1. Evaluate where you are in your career and where you want to be.
2. Identify what is no longer serving you and what you would like more of in your career.
3. Determine the steps to get where you want to go.
4. How can you drown out the noise and commit to action?

Chapter 4 - Allow yourself In

Reflections

Take the time to know yourself and understand how you process the world.

1. What are your default perceptions? Do you tend to perceive things negatively or positively throughout your day?
2. Do you have the ability to remain neutral and not attach meaning to every instance?
3. How do you deal with a challenge? Are you able to overcome a negative moment, or does it ruin your day or week?

4. How do you cultivate joy in your day?
5. What is your greatest quality? How do you show up for yourself? How would you like to show up for yourself?

Chapter 5 - Higher Power

Reflections

1. Evaluate the role of faith in your life.
2. What are the questions that you have about your current faith? Have you taken the time to explore them?
3. What gives you hope for a brighter tomorrow?
4. How do you connect with what gives you hope? How often?
5. What are the rituals that you do to nurture that connection when you are feeling low or when you are happy?

Chapter 6 - Know your Presence

Reflections

1. How do you impact the spaces you enter?
2. How do you feel in social situations? Do you feel energized? Do you feel depleted?
3. How do your friends and family describe you? Are there any characteristics you would like to work on?
4. What is the quality that people love about you? How does it impact your relationships?
5. What qualities do you value and love about yourself?

Chapter 7 - Friends and Family

Reflections

1. How do people in your life make you feel? Make a list of your family and friends.
2. How can you modify or remove those people who are depleting you from your life?
3. How does support from your family and friends look to you?
4. How do you honor those who show up for you and bring you joy? This is important to me because it's great if your family and friends are showing up for you, but how are you honoring them?

Chapter 8 - Romantic Relationships

Reflections

1. Do you know what your needs are and how do you communicate them? Do you assume that your partner knows what you want?
2. What are your boundaries, and how do you respond when they're not respected? Do you just brush it off? If you communicate boundaries without enforcing them, you have suggestions, and people will overstep them all the time.
3. How do you show up for your partner in your relationship? Maybe you don't have a partner now, but how do you show up for the people who you are seeking a relationship with or how would you like to?
4. Do you know what your partner's needs are? Have you ever asked them how they want to be loved? How do they want to be cared

for? We must acknowledge that how we want to be loved and how we define love may not always be the way someone receives love and defines love.

5. How do you want to be loved today? Reminder, you are never too much and deserve all the love that you desire.

Chapter 9 - Physical Story

Reflections

1. How can you show your body more love? What do you love most about your appearance?
2. What negative story do you tell yourself about your body? What can you start saying to yourself instead?
3. How can you implement exercise in ways that you enjoy? How many times a week can you exercise?
4. What have you tried, and why hasn't it worked?
5. How does committing to moving your body make you feel?
6. If this is an area in which you excel, take some time to acknowledge your hard work and give yourself a moment of celebration.

Chapter 10 - Health Check

Reflections

1. Evaluate what you consume daily or weekly.
2. How often do you incorporate healthy alternatives into your meal?
3. What is your favorite meal? How frequently do you eat it?

4. Pay attention to your body after you've eaten; how do you feel? Our body gives us signs when it doesn't like something, but we don't notice them because we are in a constant state of discomfort.
5. Is there something you know you are overindulging in? What is it?
6. What is your favorite healthy food? Can you find more ways to incorporate it?
7. If this is an area in which you excel, find ways to be at peace with it and celebrate yourself for all your hard work.

Chapter 11 - Environmental Shift

Reflections

1. Evaluate your external environment and places you frequent.
2. Do you feel at home when you're at home? What can you add to improve your mood? Can you add a plant or nightstand? You would be surprised how little conveniences can improve your state of mind.
3. Have you evaluated your social media? Is it curated with only things that interest you? Do you engage with content that supports your peace of mind?
4. Where and when do you feel most at peace? I ask that you don't choose to rely on a vacation because it is important that we don't get caught in destination happiness—I will be happy when I get this or when I get that. Focus on what's in front of us. We can desire things, but we shouldn't delay our happiness until we get them.
5. If this is an area where you excel, take a minute to sit in your space and express gratitude for where you are and what you have been able to do for yourself.

Chapter 12 - Maintain Your Peace

Reflections

1. What are some of the things that make you feel good about yourself, and how often do you engage in them?
2. How do you typically respond to life's challenges, and are you committed to making changes to overcome them?
3. Have you ever had a negative experience with therapy, and if so, what did you learn from it?
4. How do you deal with change, especially when it involves a loss of identity or a sense of uncertainty about the future?
5. What strategies do you have in place for seeking support when you feel overwhelmed, and how effective have they been for you in the past?
6. How do you make space for the new version of yourself as you evolve and change over time, and what are some of the challenges that come with this process?
7. In what ways can love and peace of mind protect you from life's problems, and how can you cultivate these qualities in your life?

Chapter 13 – Success Story

1. When was the last time you evaluated and questioned your definition of success? Whose story are you living?
2. How does your current definition of success align with your values and bring you peace of mind?
3. Have you ever felt unhappy or unfulfilled despite achieving what society deems as success? Reflect on that experience.

4. What aspects of your current definition of success do you want to let go of? What new aspects do you want to embrace?
5. In the quest for success, remember that your journey is uniquely yours, and it's okay to redefine success on your terms.

Chapter 14 – Redefining Success

1. How do external factors, such as familial expectations and societal pressures, influence your perception of success?
2. How can you redefine success to include personal growth, well-being, and inner peace as essential components?
3. What role does self-worth play in your definition of success? How can you redefine success from a place of self-love?
4. What values and principles do you want to guide your redefined version of success?
5. Are you open to changing your mind and exploring new paths as you redefine success? How can you give yourself permission to do so?
6. How can you honor your decisions and navigate the challenges that arise when redefining success?
7. What level of belief do you have in achieving the success you have defined?

    What can you do to strengthen those beliefs daily?
8. What dreams have you set aside or dismissed in the past due to societal pressures? How can you resurrect and pursue them now?
9. How will you take the first step towards aligning your life with your redefined version of success, starting today?

10. What actions can you commit to that will nurture your self-worth and inner peace, ensuring they remain at the core of your journey to success?
11. Take 5 minutes to envision the extraordinary possibilities that await you when you prioritize your peace and define success on your own terms.

Write down that vision and come back to it daily.

PEACE YOUR WAY TO SUCCESS AFFIRMATIONS

In this section of the book, I have included affirmations connected to each of the five parts. Feel free to use them or get inspired to create your own. Affirmations are like planting good thoughts in your mind. They help you build a positive way of thinking, moving away from doubts and scarcities towards confidence and abundance. Affirmations strengthen your positive beliefs about yourself and your abilities, helping you take the needed steps to reach your goals. They're a strong tool that helps align your thoughts, feelings, and actions, guiding you toward inner peace and achieving all you aspire to.

Finances:

1. I am capable of managing my finances wisely.
2. I attract abundance and financial prosperity into my life.
3. I am in control of my financial decisions and make choices that align with my values.
4. Money flows to me effortlessly and abundantly.
5. I release any fear or scarcity mindset around money and embrace a mindset of abundance.

6. I am grateful for the financial blessings I have and for the opportunities to grow my wealth.
7. I attract positive financial opportunities and create a stable foundation for my future.
8. My financial goals are within reach, and I am taking the necessary steps to achieve them.
9. I trust in my ability to create a healthy relationship with money and build long-term wealth.
10. I am worthy of financial success and deserve to live a life of financial freedom.
11. I release any fears or worries about money, embracing a mindset of abundance and security.

Mental Well-being:

1. I am worthy of love, joy, and inner peace.
2. I release all negative thoughts and embrace a positive mindset.
3. I am in control of my thoughts, and I choose to focus on empowering and uplifting beliefs.
4. I am resilient, and I overcome challenges with grace and ease.
5. I am at peace with myself and accept myself unconditionally.
6. My mind is calm, and I attract clarity and mental clarity into my life.
7. I prioritize self-care and nurture my mental well-being every day.
8. I let go of stress and embrace a life filled with peace and serenity.
9. I am grateful for the present moment and find joy in the little things.

10. I trust in the journey of life, knowing that everything unfolds for my highest good.
11. I am deserving of mental clarity, emotional balance, and the success that flows from a peaceful mind.

Interconnections

1. I attract loving and supportive relationships into my life.
2. I am deserving of healthy and fulfilling relationships.
3. I communicate openly and honestly, fostering deep connections with others.
4. I set clear boundaries that honor and respect my needs and well-being.
5. I am surrounded by positive and uplifting people who inspire and encourage me.
6. I forgive others and release any resentment or negativity in my relationships.
7. I attract authentic connections that align with my values and bring me joy.
8. I am a magnet for love and attract the right people into my life.
9. My relationships are filled with love, understanding, and mutual respect.
10. I am committed to nurturing and growing my relationships with love and kindness.
11. My connections with others are grounded in respect, empathy, and mutual growth.

Physical Health

1. I love and appreciate my body unconditionally.
2. My body is a temple, and I treat it with care and respect.
3. I am grateful for my body's strength, vitality, and resilience.
4. I am connected to the energy of my environment, and it supports my growth and success.
5. I listen to my body's needs and nourish it with wholesome food and regular exercise.
6. I honor my body's natural rhythms and provide it with ample rest and rejuvenation.
7. My physical environment is a reflection of my inner peace and harmony.
8. I release clutter from my surroundings and create space for clarity and serenity.
9. I embrace my unique beauty and radiate confidence from within
10. Nature nurtures my soul, and I am grateful for the beauty that surrounds me.
11. I am connected to the energy of my environment, and it supports my growth and success.

Environment:

1. My physical environment is a reflection of my inner peace and harmony.
2. I create a home that is a sanctuary of tranquility and positive energy.
3. I surround myself with objects that bring me joy and inspire creativity.

4. I am mindful of my ecological footprint and make choices that contribute to a sustainable world.
5. Nature nurtures my soul, and I spend time connecting with the natural world.
6. I release clutter from my surroundings and create space for clarity and serenity.
7. I am grateful for the beauty that surrounds me, both indoors and outdoors.
8. I create an environment that supports my well-being and promotes a sense of calm.
9. My surroundings uplift and inspire me to live a purposeful and joyful life.
10. I am connected to the energy of my environment, and it supports my growth and success.
11. I align my physical surroundings with my inner aspirations.

Peace Your Way to Success

1. I embrace peace as the foundation of my success journey.
2. I choose inner peace as the compass guiding my actions and decisions.
3. I release the need to rush and embrace the flow of progress at my own pace.
4. Peace is not the absence of challenges; it is the strength to navigate them with grace.
5. I find peace in the present moment and trust that success will unfold in its own time.
6. My success is rooted in alignment with my values and inner peace.

7. I release comparison and embrace my unique path to success, honoring my own definition.
8. I cultivate peace within myself, and it radiates into every aspect of my life and endeavors.
9. Each step I take towards my goals is an opportunity to grow in peace and self-awareness.
10. Success is not an external destination; it is a state of inner peace and fulfillment that I create.
11. I trust that peace and success are intertwined on my unique journey.
12. I release the need for external validation and find peace in my own self-worth.
13. I embrace the process of growth and learning as an essential part of my success.
14. Peace is my anchor in times of uncertainty, guiding me towards my highest potential.
15. I let go of fear and embrace peace, knowing that it paves the way for success.
16. I am deserving of success, and I attract it by cultivating inner peace and harmony.
17. Peace is my power, and it enables me to overcome obstacles and achieve my goals.
18. I find peace in celebrating both small and big victories along my journey to success.
19. I release the need for perfection and instead embrace progress and peace.
20. My success is not limited by external circumstances; I create my own peace and define my own path to success.

These affirmations serve as reminders that peace and success are interconnected, and by nurturing inner peace, you can create a solid foundation for achieving your goals. Repeat these affirmations regularly and allow them to uplift and inspire you as you navigate your unique journey towards success.

MESSAGE FROM THE AUTHOR

Your peace is your power, and it is non-negotiable. Everything you aspire to experience is intricately tied to your unwavering commitment to showing up for yourself. This book has been carefully crafted to serve as your guide in defining your unique story, reclaiming your inner peace, and pursuing success on your own terms.

As you continue along your journey, please keep in mind that self-discovery and self-care are ongoing processes. They demand your love, patience, and understanding. You may encounter moments of doubt or uncertainty but have faith in your ability to navigate them with grace and resilience.

Above all else, never underestimate the profound power of your own story. You possess the capacity to redefine success, to rewrite the story as many times as necessary, and to construct a life that aligns with your values and aspirations. Trust yourself and choose the path that supports your well-being and feels true to you.

Remember, your peace is not something to be compromised or sacrificed for the sake of comfort, doubt, or societal pressures. It is a precious and integral facet of your being. Embrace it, safeguard it, and allow it to illuminate the way toward a life of true fulfillment and authentic success.

May this book serve as a guiding light, reminding you that peace is the compass that will lead you to the ease and abundance you deserve. Embrace the journey, celebrate your progress, and always bear in mind that peace is your birthright.

I extend my heartfelt gratitude for joining me on this transformative exploration and inviting meaningful change. May peace be the driving force behind your every step, and may success unfold in ways that surpass your wildest dreams.

Peace Always,

Kenisha

ACKNOWLEDGMENT

I want to express my heartfelt gratitude to the incredible individuals who played a pivotal role in making "Peace Your Way to Success" a reality. This journey of self-discovery, patience, grace, and faith has been an incredible adventure, and I am deeply thankful for your unwavering support. To those who directly coached and mentored me, like Jasmine Womack, and those who joined me for coffee or tea chats, or simply shared the space of a café, your presence fueled my inspiration. Your encouragement and insights have been invaluable.

A special thank you goes out to my partner, who stood by me through the late nights, the ups and downs, the constants, and the changes. Thank you for your love and support.

To all those who loved me through every twist and turn of this journey, I extend my heartfelt thanks. Though I cannot possibly name all the wonderful souls who contributed to this book, I would like to mention a few whose impact was profound:

Stella Naggenda - The love and growth in our friendship mean the world to me. Naturally, you were the very first person I confided in about my intention to write this book, and your unwavering support and presence have been a constant source of strength and inspiration by my side.

Karyn Hanson - Your unwavering love and support, especially as I ventured into the realm of social media, have been instrumental in this journey.

Mom and Dad - I appreciate your openness in allowing me to share my truth, even when it may not have been the easiest perspective to hear. Your support means everything to me.

To my siblings, nephews, and my niece - Your love and presence in my life is one of the most important things to me, and I hope you always know how deeply I care for you. Thank you for your unconditional love and support.

Mama - Your unwavering belief in me, without a hint of doubt, has been a constant source of motivation. Your support has not only been my guiding light but also the warm embrace that has carried me through this journey.

Thank you, each and every one of you, for being a part of this incredible journey. Your love and support have made all the difference.

Peace Always,

Kenisha

AUTHOR BIO

Kenisha Hanson is a Personal Development Coach and wellness expert who has dedicated her life to helping individuals navigate the challenges of personal growth and find inner peace and fulfillment. Born in Canada and educated at the prestigious University of York in the United Kingdom and Toronto Metropolitan University, Kenisha's journey into the realm of personal development was shaped by her own remarkable experiences and profound transformations.

After obtaining her Master of Science in Psychology, Kenisha embarked on a career in the mental health and justice sector where she now also coaches senior leaders to advance their careers and gain clarity in their professional paths. However, her own life took an unexpected turn when she received a devastating diagnosis of stage 4 Hodgkin's lymphoma at the age of thirty. This life-altering event shook her to the core, coming on the heels of her mother's diagnosis with a rare autoimmune disorder that left her completely paralyzed. It was during this challenging period that Kenisha embarked on a deeper journey of self-discovery and self-care.

Kenisha dove into various training, meditation practices, and spiritual exploration to understand herself on a deeper level and find the strength to navigate her own circumstances. This inward journey became the catalyst for her personal growth and transformation, inspiring her to share her wisdom and insights with others.

Living a holistic lifestyle to support her own wellbeing, Kenisha is no stranger to hardship and unpredictable circumstances. Yet, through her unique personal outlook, which has become a signature framework, she gracefully navigates the world while prioritizing her peace and wellbeing. Her teachings are simple yet highly effective, grounded in self-reflection and empowerment.

As a deeply introspective coach, Kenisha helps individuals connect to their inner voice, unravel their true selves, and gain clarity on their desires and aspirations. She understands the challenges of not feeling ready and the importance of finding inner peace and fulfillment in our lives. Kenisha's mission is to inspire people to live in alignment with their values and goals, urging them to prioritize themselves and embrace the present moment.

Kenisha's teachings transcend any specific domain, as she believes that true transformation starts from within. Whether it's personal finance, career advancement, nurturing relationships, or embracing a fulfilling lifestyle, she firmly believes that self-reflection and self-awareness form the foundation of our peace and happiness. By cultivating a deeper connection to ourselves, we can enhance our interactions with others and truly experience the richness of life.

These days, you can often find Kenisha savoring life's simple pleasures—taking contemplative strolls, unwinding at a nearby café, or connecting with friends over afternoon tea. Committed to her own ongoing personal development, Kenisha not only lives by the principles she advocates but also opens up about the authentic journey. Through her work, she aims to demonstrate that peace is both attainable and fundamental in nurturing the life you've always envisioned.

Through her captivating and relatable approach, Kenisha Hanson has touched the lives of countless individuals, empowering them to uncover their authentic selves, overcome obstacles, and thrive in all aspects of life. As you embark on your own transformative journey, allow Kenisha's guidance to illuminate the path, inspire change, and guide you towards a life of purpose, fulfillment, and self-discovery.

Connect with Author

Make sure to grab the accompanying resource guide, designed to enhance your exploration of the concepts covered in this book at: www.peaceandsuccess.com .

Join the community and connect with me on social media: @thekenishahanson.

Visit the website and subscribe to the mailing list for early access to upcoming events, exclusive merchandise, and valuable resources.

Stay informed and inspired!

Notes

Notes

Notes

Notes

Notes

SYNOPSIS

Without peace, success is just an empty achievement.

In today's fast-paced society, it's easy to overlook the importance of self-care and inner peace in the pursuit of productivity and success. Kenisha Hanson, a wellness expert, and cancer survivor, challenges this notion in her book *Peace Your Way to Success*. Through her personal experience and expertise in personal development, Hanson encourages readers to prioritize their own well-being and find fulfillment in their lives. The book offers readers a roadmap to define their own success story and navigate life's inevitable challenges. By prioritizing self-care and inner peace, readers can not only achieve their goals, but also lead a more fulfilling life. *Peace Your Way to Success* is a transformative read for those seeking to find balance and harmony in their pursuit of success.

In *Peace Your Way to Success*, you will learn how to:

- Evaluate various areas of your life to determine how they support you or deplete you.
- Create effective boundaries by understanding your needs.
- Equip yourself with tools to navigate inevitable hardships.

- Obtain the clarity you need to define your success story and pursue your goals.
- Show up for yourself every single day.

Cultivating peace of mind is not a luxury but a fundamental necessity for achieving true fulfillment and success in all aspects of life. Whether you're a high-achieving professional, a student, a parent, or simply looking to improve your overall well-being, *Peace Your Way to Success* provides the tools you need to achieve your goals and live a happier, more satisfying life.

Kenisha Hanson is an empowering force that makes you feel capable of achieving anything you set your mind to. As a wellness expert, coach and cancer survivor with a Master of Science in Psychology, Kenisha brings a grounded perspective to her work. She radiates kindness and embodies inner peace, serving as an inspiration to those around her. Kenisha has a unique ability to strike the perfect balance between assertion and compassion, empowering her clients to feel confident and in control of their lives.

www.ingramcontent.com/pod-product-compliance
Lightning Source LLC
Chambersburg PA
CBHW021110080526
44587CB00010B/463